Welcome to

2015

First there was Kevin Pietersen saying in his controversial autobiography that he was bullied, a claim that deserves to get him a good kicking the next time he's in the dressing room.

Then there was Roy Keane slaughtering Fergie in his controversial autobiography and saying he should never have apologied to him, a claim that deserves to get him the Irish equivalent of a knighthood (four cans of Guinness on the house).

But now, just in time for Christmas, or Easter if you've bought this from a knock-off book shop in 2015, comes the BOOK, er, GLOSSY MAGAZINE (THAT WOULD BE A CARDBOARD ANNUAL IF WE COULD AFFORD CARDBOARD) OF THE YEAR.

For an incredible 11th year, The Kop Annual is back. And, just to be different, we've called it The Kop Annual 2015. F**k knows what we'll call the next one.

If you've never seen The Kop Annual before then can you please place this copy of it just below your chin, in line with your chest, allowing you to read on while holding your head in shame.

The Kop Annual 2015 features the best bits from The Kop Magazine – our monthly unofficial Liverpool FC magazine that celebrates its 20th anniversary in 2015 – and loads of brand new content.

You'll hopefully have gathered by now that we're all about fun and the lighter side of football in our annual, but The Kop Magazine features a mixture of hard-hitting comment, unique analysis, honestly held opinion, exclusive competitions plus plenty of irreverence and laughs along the way. So let's get on with the laughing.

Brendan Rodgers personally kept Southampton FC afloat last summer by signing half their team so our resident cartoonist PAK has paid tribute to the new boys the Reds shipped in on our front cover.

And, just to check if you're reading this, the first person who tweets us (@TheKopMagazine) to explain the relevance of the flags on the back cover will win a mystery prize. Seriously.

In this year's Kop Annual we reveal how Steven Gerrard has become obsessed with kissing cameras after his goalscoring exploits at Old Trafford, we try to find a new partner for Danny Sturridge in a Strictly Come DANcing special and we reveal the alternatives Everton could've plastered on the side of Goodison Park.

We've got a poster tribute to a World Cup winner, our Google Maps 'Whose Ground is it Anyway?' quiz goes on tour again and old favourites such as You Ask, We Answer and Kop Karaoke get another airing.

You'll have to draw on your Liverpool knowledge for 'Guess the Goal' and to mark the forthcoming 10th anniversary of the Reds' fifth European Cup triumph we present to you Quiztanbul – a collection of 50 Istanbul questions that will test everyone and anyone who thinks they know the lot about events on May 25, 2005. Enjoy.

#UnnecessaryHashtag #TurnThePageThenKnobhead

Words: Boyzone
Design/editing/writing: Chris McLoughlin, Roy Gilfoyle, Michael McGuinness, Colin Sumpter, Glen Hind, Alison Barkley, Lee Ashun and Gary Gilliland
Photographic credits: Trinity Mirror, PA Pics. **Illustrations:** Peter King. **Printers:** PCP.
JFT96

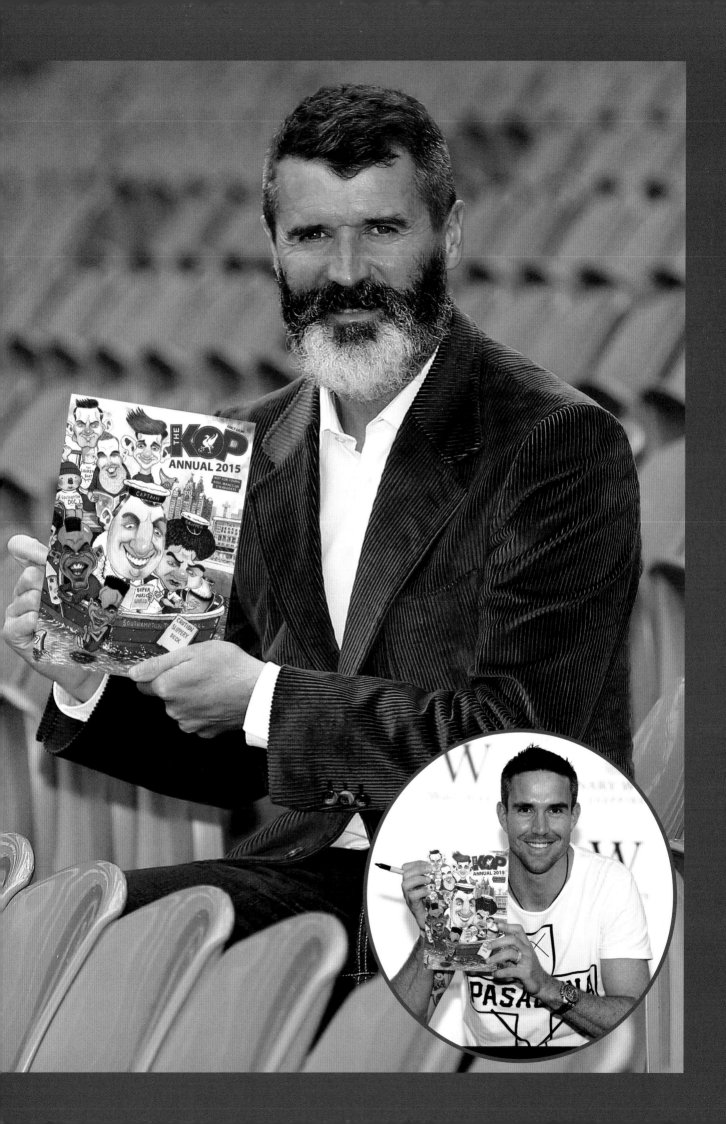

DILDO LO MEJOR

Contents

QUIZTANBUL

STEVIE LAX
'You'll definitely go again'

UNFLAVORED POWDER
GRIT FREE

Warning: Seeing a Man
Shitty may cause irritation

38 doses a season   NET WT 17.9 OZ (510g)

More stuff wot's in the Annual

LIFE WITH A LENS

BY STEVIE G

The story of my struggle to control an addiction that has taken over my life...

I used to be a fairly ordinary footballer

The only things I used to kiss were the club crest...

...major trophies...

...my beautiful family...

...and the occasional team-mate

Then one day everything changed. We played the Mancs at Old Trafford and I was tingling as if something special was close right from the off...

LIFE WITH A LENS BY STEVIE G

I won a penalty just before half time...

I stuck it away and went to celebrate with our fans – and then it happened...

...I kissed the TV camera. I don't know why I did it. Maybe I wanted to show the fans at home how much I love them. Maybe it was the excitement of going 2-1 up. Maybe I just wanted to piss off the lad in the second row who was giving me the Vs. Whatever the reason, I enjoyed that kiss and I knew I wanted to do it again

So, I did do it again. The following year in the same place. And I was so confident of scoring I was looking to make sure the camera was ready for me as I tucked in the penalty

That's when the addiction started to take hold. Some weeks I'd find myself in Dixons every day, just so I could be around cameras

Hey mate, how's anyone supposed to kiss, errr, look at the cameras when they're behind glass?!

The next thing you know I was blowing kisses to speed cameras just so they knew someone appreciated their work

I never tried to kiss this camera though. Too many painful memories

I got quite excited when Roy told me Dave the cameraman wanted to meet me, but he forgot his equipment so there was no way I was kissing him

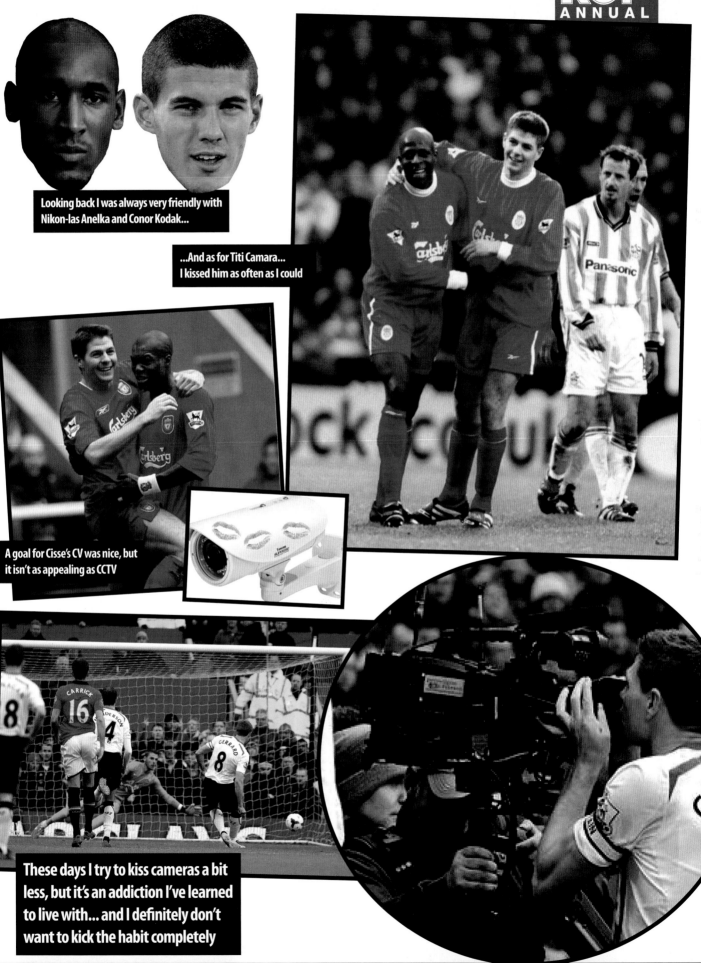

clocked

Another year, another set of celebrities have been spotted by eagle-eyed Kopites – from Les Dennis to Ian Ayre and Victoria Wood...

Goodman's dancing all the way to the Albert Dock

Check out Les

Robbie Fowler loves a bit of boxing

Victoria Wood caught in the act

You can't keep Jamie away from Anfield

Luis and Sofia Suarez going into BMI Sefton Hospital, Kenilworth Road, Blundellsands.

Blackpool boss Paul Ince loudly asking for table service in the Devon Doorway pub, Heswall.

Kenny Dalglish walking into the Thistle Hotel, Glasgow, for a Billy McNeill tribute dinner.

South Sydney Rabbitohs rugby league prop forward George Burgess drinking in the Oast House restaurant, Spinningfields, Manchester.

Steven Pienaar sat in a chair inside Johnny Goggles opticians, North John Street.

Luis Suarez driving down Allerton Road in what looked very much like Pepe Reina's white Escalade.

Ian Ayre straining his eyes looking down Chapel Street at 8am one morning before heading into the LFC offices.

Everton's Gerard Deulofeu and Joel Robles walking past Goldsmith's jewellers, Liverpool One.

Steven Pienaar

Les Dennis looking a little harassed doing his weekly big shop in Sainsbury's, Cheadle.

Jamie Carragher and his son James in the Main Stand car park.

Ex-Warrington RLFC stand-off Lee Briers heading into Anfield.

Robbie Fowler watching Liam Smith, Derry Mathews and Paul Butler boxing at the ECHO Arena.

Jordan Henderson, Danny Sturridge and Zaf Iqbal leaving Spire Hospital, Greenbank Road.

Kenny Dalglish walking down Brook Street, close to the passport office, on the same day he did a book signing at the Liverpool One official LFC club shop.

Sofie Munthe, wife of Daniel Agger, in St Peter's Square, Manchester.

Ricky Tomlinson joining in a UNITE protest next to the Ken Dodd statue in Lime Street Station.

Glen Johnson, with his family at Farmer Ted's near Formby, looking a bit befuddled when a young Liverpool fan told him "I've got you in Match Attax."

Tranmere's Andy Robinson watching his lad play in the Merseyside Under-14s trials at Walton Soccer Centre.

Former Everton midfielder Graham Stuart watching Swansea v Everton in The Park pub, Birkdale.

Paul Wellens, Jon Wilkin and several other members of the St Helens rugby league team drinking in the Fly In The Loaf, Hardman Street.

Kenny Dalglish walking through the Main Stand car park.

Canterbury Bulldogs' Everton-supporting James Graham walking down North John Street.

Brad Jones, Dani Lawrence and their son Nico having a meal in Est Est, Aigburth.

Ian Callaghan heading past the Slug & Lettuce, North John Street.

Brad Jones

Glasgow boy Kenny Dalglish

Amanda's definitely fit

Ayre with a stare

John W Henry and Linda Pizzuti having a meal in San Carlo, Castle Street.

Amanda Harrington in her gym gear putting money into a parking meter on Old Hall Street.

Raheem Sterling getting off the London Euston to Liverpool Lime Street train and diving into a taxi.

Robbie Fowler having a cup of tea in the Premier Lounge, Langtree Park.

Former AC Milan striker Luther Blissett, wearing a flat cap.

Rob Jones stood in the Langtree Park players' tunnel waiting to have a word with members of Liverpool's Under-18s side.

Victoria Wood standing by the side of Liverpool Town Hall during a break from filming Foyle's War.

Former Aston Villa player Pat Heard, who was on the bench during their 1982 European Cup final success, drinking a pint of John Smiths in The Arkles.

Peter Hooton heading down the stairs in block 206 of The Kop.

Jon Flanagan having a night out in Santa Chupitos, Slater Street.

Howard Gayle carrying Heron carrier bags walking past Home & Bargain, Allerton Road.

Len Goodman chilling out in Costa Coffee, Albert Dock.

Daniel Agger lost his place in the Liverpool starting XI in 2013/14, with Kolo Toure, Mamadou Sakho and Martin Skrtel monopolising the centre-back positions. Tiago Ilori came in, went out on loan, came back and, er, went out on loan again with Dejan Lovren's arrival making the pair even odder pieces in the defensive jigsaw

THE KOP MOLE

Digging out the best of the Kop goss and dirt on our rivals from 2014...

STICKER SMILE ON YER FACE WITH THESE PHOTO FAILS

THE oldschoolpanini.com website showcases football stickers from back in the day and they took things to a whole new level of hilarity when unearthing these French gems from just after Euro '92.

It shows that Eric Cantona was framed long before Matthew Simmons (allegedly) insulted his mother, that Emmanuel Petit was equally at home in the midfield engine room with a Sierra as he was with Vieira, and that Basile Boli had absolutely no idea how to sit on a chair properly.

But best of all was the conclusive proof that Laurent Blanc did indeed play alongside Gary Pallister despite the record books claiming he only signed for Manchester United three years after Pally's departure from Old Trafford.

Is it a bird? Is it a plane? No, it's a Geordie in a daft suit

GOOD to see that Newcastle United found haway around the various objections to wearing the Wonga logo with their new home kit for the 2014/15 season.

Can't see Mike Ashley fitting his incredible bulk into one though – they're only available up to size XL and he might not appreciate the chants of 'dinner dinner dinner dinner Fatman' that will come his way...

No corners taken in customising of this LFC shirt

I'M all for recycling, but it's about time this Kopite – pictured at Yankee Stadium for the pre-season win against Man City – got himself a new Liverpool shirt.

Still, it looks better than it must've done this time last year when he presumably tried to cover up the name of Liverpool's former number nine with the word Aspas...

BRUCE MERCH JUST A SPLASH IN THE PAN

HULL City's dream of winning a first FA Cup went down the pan at Wembley but at least Tigers supporters got the opportunity to buy some bog-standard memorabilia.

Local bathroom manufacturer Ideal Standard produced this commemorative toilet seat, featuring Steve Bruce's head inside the lid, before auctioning it off for charity.

If the flush buyer was a fella then it'll mean he no longer has an excuse for peeing on the floor as when you've got a head as big as Bruce's to aim at you surely can't miss.

UNITED'S CHANCES LOOK REMOTE

WHEN sky launched their set of club-branded remote controls last year, it raised a number of questions.

Do Evertonians have less channels to view than everyone else because they refuse to press the red button or, after the derby, any channel starting four zero?

Are any Tottenham fans stupid enough to pay £29.99 for one when all they're getting is a standard Sky remote control with a sticker of the club crest on the front?

Will Liverpool automatically charge a 90p booking fee every time a Kopite presses 'box office?'

And are Sky going to bring out branded versions for every Premier League club or just stick to the big seven?

Arsenal
The Arsenal Sky+HD remote is the ultimate accessory for every Gunner.
£29.99
+ £2.00 delivery — Buy

Chelsea
Can't make it to Stamford Bridge? Then watch the match with this Chelsea branded Sky+HD remote.
£29.99
+ £2.00 delivery — Buy

Everton
Support Everton this season with this exclusive Sky+HD remote.
£29.99
+ £2.00 delivery — Buy

Liverpool
Watch your favourite team play with this Liverpool branded Sky+HD remote.
£29.99
+ £2.00 delivery — Buy

Manchester City
Show you're a true MCFC supporter with this the City branded Sky+HD remote.
£29.99
+ £2.00 delivery — Buy

Newcastle
Become the ultimate NUFC fan with this Newcastle branded Sky+HD remote.
£29.99
+ £2.00 delivery — Buy

Tottenham Hotspur
Every Spurs fan should have this great remote to tune into all the big matches.
£29.99
+ £2.00 delivery — Buy

FIFA GAME NEEDS A FACELIFT

IF Roy Hodgson was ever considering having Botox or a facelift then surely EA Sports' 2014 FIFA World Cup Brazil has put him off – unless he wants to look like Steve McClaren with slightly more hair and a hamster's cheek pouch.

Raheem Sterling might also be wondering when he turned into a young Patrick Kluivert (honestly, that's meant to be Sterling), but by far the most shocking thing about 2014 FIFA World Cup Brazil is the list of England players who made it into the squad ahead of Jordan Henderson when the game was released.

No offence to EA Sports, but even Hodgson wouldn't pick Jake Livermore and Scott Parker ahead of Hendo!

SQUAD			
⊗	RM	30	R. Sterling
	RM	37	A. Lennon
	LB	34	K. Gibbs
	CDM	40	S. Parker
	CB	41	R. Shawcross
	RM	35	A. Johnson
	CB	32	S. Caulker
	CDM	38	J. Livermore
	LB	31	R. Bertrand
	CAM	42	J. Shelvey
	GK	43	J. Butland
	CB	44	S. Taylor
▶ DONE			

Average league finishing position

Figures are for teams to have played in every season in the football league since 1958

Team	Position
Liverpool	4.96
Manchester United	5.27
Arsenal	5.82
Tottenham	8.6
Everton	8.75
Chelsea	11.64
West Ham	14.82
Aston Villa	14.95
Manchester City	15.27
Newcastle	15.93
Leeds	17.22
Nottingham Forest	19.38
Southampton	20.16
Ipswich	20.53
WBA	20.98
Leicester	21.27
Blackburn	23.56
Sunderland	23.58
Wolves	24.07
Middlesbrough	24.18

WE'RE THE BEST... EVEN WHEN WE'RE AVERAGE!

A STATISTICAL analysis of every club to have played in every season of the Football League since it was extended to 92 clubs in 1958/59 was conducted by The People and Liverpool came out top on average league finishes.

The Reds also finished top in terms of the fewest goals conceded (2,125 – 330 less than anyone else) and second in terms of total points (3,541), average points per season (63.48) and goals scored (3,776).

And the worst club to have been following for the last 55 years?

Coventry City, who have collected the fewest points (2,630), have the worst points-per-season average (47.82) and only have Stoke City below them when it comes to goals scored (2,959).

Must have made those 70-mile round trips to Northampton to see home games last season all the more enthralling, eh?

H-BOMB DROPPED

TWO questions remain unanswered about this cringeworthily-titled 'Super Kewell' magazine.

Did they use the word 'bomb' on the cover because they knew that's what his career would do when he moved to Liverpool?

And did Harry's fans pay him the ultimate tribute by removing it from their walls half-way through any cup finals he was playing in?

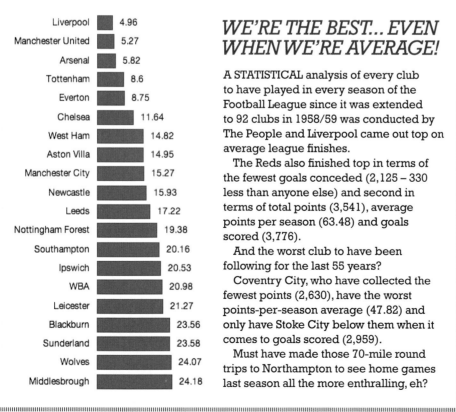

AS A HOTEL GROUP PLANS TO OPEN SHANKLY-THEMED ACCOMMODATION IN LIVERPOOL, THE KOP ANNUAL CAN EXCLUSIVELY REVEAL THE WEBSITE OF A HOTEL THAT IS SURE TO MAKE THE PEOPLE HAPPY

The Shankly Hotel

Part of the Redisson group ©

Destination

Liverpool
Glenbuck
Melwood
Wembley

Check in date

01/12/1959

Check out date

12/07/1974

Special requests

Anfield-facing room
Newspaper (but not S*n)
5am training alarm call
Guaranteed 'Silent Knight'

What guests said about us:

'After a lovely stay, having to go home was like walking to the electric chair'

'There's only two hotels I'd stay in – The Shankly Hotel and The Shankly Hotel Reserve Inn'

'The staff made it clear they believed in a Holy Trinity of a nice room, five-star service and 110% effort from everyone. Although they made it clear the customer is there to sign the cheques'

Accommodation

Range of suites including:
- Top floor Anfield Suite
- Sir Roger Honeymoon Suite
- Cellar-level room for undesirable guests named The Bitter Suite

Every room has 7ft-long Yeatsie beds, 'professional' carpets and an Anfield Iron

Every room equipped with easy-pull curtains in case Everton match breaks out outside your room

Facilities

TV rooms and sports bar showing football 24/7 including Rochdale Reserves making it the ideal location for an anniversary break

Reuben's Recuperation Room – where aches, pains and cruciate knee ligament injuries can be repaired in minutes

Special guests picked up directly from airport

Dine in

Enjoy chef's special range of soups. They're all delicious, but the leek is our bread and butter

Free steak starter with every meal and special 'Flying Pig' bacon with breakfast

Every table equipped with movable cutlery, condiments and salt and pepper pots that can be arranged in any formation

Management reserves the right to eject guests who fail to turn up for five-a-side training. Discounts given to guests who don't overeat or lose their Scottish accents

Whose ground is it anyway?

As far as we know, Google Street View was set up so we could nick their pictures and turn them into a Kop Annual quiz. Why else would they stick a camera on the roof of a car and drive past football grounds when they could just buy a photo of Dean Court from Bournemouth's club shop? Eddie Howe, sorry, anyhow, Who's Ground is it Anyway is simple to play. Just look at the Google Street Map photo and the hint we've given you about the last time Liverpool played there and name the ground. Remember, the odd one might no longer be in use these days...

1 Liverpool's last game here: 2014

2 Liverpool's last game here: 1959

QUINTILES

3

Liverpool's last game here: 2013

?

SEASON TICKETS NOW ON SALE
BUY EARLY FOR BEST PRICES!

4 Liverpool's last game here: 2001

?

5

Liverpool's last game here: 2012

6 Liverpool's last game here: 2004

7

Liverpool's last game here: 2014

8 Liverpool's last game here: 2007

9 Liverpool's last game here: 2009

10 Liverpool's last game here: 2014

ANSWERS: (All correct on November 1, 2014): Etihad Stadium, Man City.
2. Ninian Park, Cardiff City. 3. Madejski Stadium, Reading. 4. Prenton Park,
Tranmere Rovers. 5. Molineux, Wolverhampton Wanderers. 6. Huish Park,
Yeovil Town. 7. Cardiff City Stadium, Cardiff City. 8. Vicarage Road, Watford.
9. Riverside Stadium, Middlesbrough. 10. White Hart Lane, Tottenham Hotspur.

THE KOP MOLE'S PAPARAZZI PICS

When it comes to getting those highly sought after snaps, the Kop Mole is always one step ahead of the game. Over the last 12 months football's most famous gossip columnist has given Kop Magazine readers exclusive after exclusive. Here he talks us through some of his best pics of 2014

FORMER Reds midfielder Don Hutchison proved he takes his punditry with Premier League TV and Al Jazeera very seriously by posting this photo of himself getting his nails done.

Judging by the nail technician's face mask he should probably get some deodorant too.

Hutch isn't the only ex-footballer turned TV analyst who takes his appearance seriously before going on air.

Glenn Hoddle sends his hair off to be weaved through a loom 48 hours before Champions League nights on Sky and Mark Lawrenson is oiled down an hour before Match of the Day 2 in order to get into whichever garish shirt that doesn't fit him for that evening's show.

DON Hutchison's dog should count itself lucky.

The last time he was pictured half naked he only had a Budweiser label on and it wasn't positioned on his chest.

Is this photo of Harry Kewell posing in a pair of Politix undercrackers part of an advertising campaign, er, down under?

Or is this photo of Harry Kewell taken by a physio after he dislocated his shoulder trying to put his boxer shorts on?

It's the fourth time he's been pictured in briefs, the others being his brief appearances in Istanbul 2005, Cardiff 2006 and Athens 2007...

BRAD Jones has evidently seen more action off the pitch than on it if this photo of Dani Lawrence was anything to go by, but his missus isn't the only one with a Middlesbrough connection known to have walked around with a bloated tummy.

Unfortunately for ex-Boro midfielder Jamie Pollock, though, he couldn't blame being pregnant.

Still, at least he can fill a couple of those empty seats at The Riverside these days.

On his own.

GOOD to see that Liverpool keep the JFT96 message in the minds of their players even when they're relaxing by having it printed on the red baize of the pool table down at Melwood.

Perhaps they should also print it on the pool tables down at David Duckenfield and Norman Bettison's local pubs as a reminder that with each piece of evidence that emerges they look increasingly snookered.

IT isn't just Manchester United that have undergone a massive change since Alex Ferguson quit as manager.

Instead of the hairdryer treatment, Fergie will just be using the hairdryer now that he's a woman.

At least we finally know why he really stepped down now – having a sex change at the age of 72 would've simply been too risky with Wayne Rooney in his squad.

MARTIN Skrtel was forced to have his head stapled to stem the flow of blood after a clash in Liverpool's 2013/14 FA Cup fourth round win at Bournemouth.

All credit to him for continuing to play, but given he's had 75% of his body tattooed shouldn't he have laughed off the odd head staple rather than wince in pain?

GARY NEVILLE? ON THE BIG SCREEN? WE'D RATHER SIT THROUGH AN IN-DEPTH INTERVIEW CONDUCTED BY GARTH CROOKS. FORGET 'CLASS OF '92', THIS IS A FILM WITH MORE BLOCKBUSTER POTENTIAL. IT COULD BE A REAL TEAR-JERKER FOR REDS WHO LIVED THROUGH THE PAIN FIRST TIME AROUND THOUGH

PAUL
STEWART

NICKY
TANNER

ISTVAN
KOZMA

GRAEME
SOUNESS

MIKE
HOOPER

TORBEN
PIECHNIK

THE GASH OF '92

THE MEN WHO DESTROYED AN EMPIRE

★ ★ ★ *I owe everything to these guys* – **Whisky Nose magazine**

Luis Suarez became the fastest player to hit 20 Premier League goals a single season in 2014, and would go on to beat God's record over a full* campaign too… *Er, 'full' other than the ocassional ban for nibbling an opponent

THE KOP Challenge ...best of

Jan spot on again

2015 marks the 12th birthday of the Kop Challenge and you're still sending in your Reds-related holiday snaps from more places than ever before.

We've broken new ground recently as the Challenge soared past more than 100 countries visited. Some of those new far, foreign lands feature here, along with a photo with a Liverpool legend, and a cheeky pic behind enemy lines.

More of the best Kop Challenge entries are on pages 68/69. Alright then...

BIG Jan Molby used to stand in the centre of the park spreading passes about so it was no surprise to see him stood with professor Roy Park spreading his fingers out in one of the Anfield suites.

The great Dane even positioned himself close to a Carlsberg sign, although quite why Liverpool appear to be serving it in tea cups is a mystery, unless Graeme Souness was behind the bar ready to throw them at people.

Until Steven Gerrard recently beat him, Molby was the Reds' most prolific penalty taker ever, scoring 42 of the 45 spot-kicks he took to spark rumours that he was actually German. His record is in complete contrast to that of another great signing from Ajax, Luis Suarez, who missed two out of two, sparking rumours that he is English. Or Charlie Adam in disguise.

Towards the end of his Liverpool career, Big Jan was clearly hampered by carrying excess lumps of useless flesh, but in his defence it wasn't his fault that Paul Stewart was selected to play alongside him in midfield.

His ability to fire shots on goal at speed was matched only by his ability to drive a car at speed when the police were chasing him and during the six-week spell he spent in Kirkham Open Prison he recalls a five-a-side game in which he nutmegged a Manc who was so angry that he got him up against a wall.

Good practice for when Roy Keane signed for United a few years later, then.

from **Anfield, Liverpool**

Neil swings into Dubai - good Evans that's high up

DAVID Moores almost sold Liverpool Football Club to Dubai International Capital in 2007 but stalled on the deal after discovering they had already drawn up a seven-year exit strategy to sell the club.

People living on the top floor of Dubai's Burj Khalifa tower also have a seven-year exit strategy in place for when the lifts are out of order as that's how long it takes to climb down the stairs.

Standing at over 828 metres high, the Burj Khalifa is the tallest building in the world and also claims to have the most stories – a fact disputed by staff at Liverpool Central Library and readers of the Sunday Times. It's certainly a long way down from the top, but that's enough about Manchester United's final league position last season.

Grimsby-based Kopite Neil Evans could see the heavens from the 124th floor observation deck of the Burj Khalifa and took The Kop Challenge while he was up there. It was the highest we've been since going on a night out with One Direction.

Neil also gave a five-fingered salute on a Dubai golf course, appropriately on the tee of the 5th hole which has a notorious, sloping green that often leaves golfers facing 'a Dennis Wise' – a nasty little five-footer – to save par.

from **Dubai, United Arab Emirates**

In Istanbul, we done The Kop Challenge

IT'S hard to believe that it will be 10 years in May since Liverpool won the Champions League in Istanbul but plans are already underway to mark the anniversary in style.

Steven Gerrard is planning to lift ol' Big Ears in Berlin on June 6, Jerzy Dudek is off to the Polish border to block anything the Ukrainians throw at him and Josemi will spend the entire summer inside the Anfield museum to get on any photographs visitors want with the European Cup.

UEFA have even offered to hold a reunion dinner in a more accessible location than the Ataturk Stadium was in 2005 although they've yet to confirm that Chernobyl is available.

Wherever the dinner is held, Harry Kewell is expected to limp away long before the main course is served.

Istanbul has naturally been a popular location for Kop Challenge entries and another Red to give five-fingered salutes there was Centenary Stand season ticket holder Ray Smith and his wife Ann during a Mediterranean cruise stop-off.

Jose Mourinho and his Chelsea squad had also booked onto the liner so they could finally see what Istanbul was like but had to cancel the trip after discovering they weren't allowed to park the bus in front of Mark Schwarzer's cabin.

Chelsea have been accused of playing boring football and as soon as we're able to stay awake during one of their games we'll tell you if the criticism is justified.

from **Istanbul, Turkey**

Sunley excells himself... again!

DARREN Sunley's one-man mission to take The Kop Challenge in every country – even the ones Russia haven't invaded yet – continues apace and the much-travelled Red, a description that can also be used to describe Fergie's nose, has given five-fingered salutes in four new countries.

Indonesia has a population of 246.9 million, the type of number Damien Comolli could get two strikers for, but despite seemingly the whole nation supporting Liverpool we've never had a Kop Challenge photo from there until now.

Darren gave a five-fingered salute from the top of Kintamani, overlooking the volcano and Lake Batur, in Bali, a beautiful island named after a type of dancing people do in tights.

Cheryl Cole's nickname is 'volcano' – she chucked out Ash as well – a joke we've been waiting to make since they split up in 2010 in order to let the dust settle first.

Darren picked Dili in East Timor next and took The Kop Challenge in front of the Cristo Rei monument, the second biggest of its kind in the world after the one Cristiano Ronaldo has of himself in his back garden.

East Timor was known as Portuguese Timor until 1975 when it was decolonised, which sounds like it must have been a painful operation. For those of you who don't know where the country lies geographically, it's to the east of West Timor.

Taiwan also makes a Kop Challenge debut this month thanks to Darren's five-fingered salute overlooking Sun Moon Lake outside Syuanguang Temple, Asian cousin of Shirley.

Technically part of China, Taiwan's biggest industry is producing Made in Taiwan clothing labels, although rarely do the garments attached to them indicate where they were made.

Here in the UK, we have Made in Chelsea – a surprisingly popular TV programme about where parked buses are manufactured.

Our fourth new country is Liechtenstein. Despite sounding like something the dog has done to your collection of two-pint glasses, Liechtenstein is the richest German-speaking country in the world, the only nation to be completely surrounded by the Alps and has a population of 35,000 – just 15,000 more people than the total attendance of SPFL games on weekends when Celtic are away.

Darren is pictured taking the Kop Challenge outside the parliament building in Vaduz which was donated to the country by an anonymous Swiss chocolate manufacturer.

Also featuring on Darren's tour was the Anfield Sports Pub in Lucerne, Switzerland, and the Concorde Museum in Barbados, which only allows visitors in with one bag and serves drinks in containers of 100ml or less in the cafe.

Concorde flew for 27 years before being sadly retired in 2003 before it could appear on Channel 4's Embarrassing Bodies to see if there was anything that could be done about its drooping nose.

from **All over, basically**

East Timor

Bali

Barbados

Switzerland

Taiwan

Liechtenstein

REDS TO OPEN OFFICE IN LONDON

Bleedin' ell, gov. The Mickey Mousers have only gone and announced they're opening a new office dahn sarf in that there London. Would you Adam and Eve it? Ian Ayre reckons it'll help Liverpool secure new sponsors, but he didn't say where the office is so we've had a butcher's hook around England's second city to see if we can spot the club's new commercial home...

Big Brother star Dappy had a big breakfast

cl⊙cked

Kevin Kilbane walking down Old Hall Street close to the William Hill bookies.

Purple Aki queuing up at the Liverpool ECHO's reception desk.

Neil Fitzmaurice in the Lower Centenary Stand car park.

John Barnes in the Lower Centenary Stand getting absolutely mobbed.

Joe Cole, wearing a woolly hat and keeping his nut down as he walked out of the Kop.

Jamie Carragher, on his phone, walking down North John Street, Cook Street and Brunswick Street, er, not that we were following him!

Ian Callaghan getting on a train at Moorfields.

Luis Suarez paying for unspecified goods in Mamas and Papas, Liverpool One.

Tony Hibbert driving down Liverpool Road, Formby, in a blue BMW.

David Fairclough, walking with a slight limp, close to McGuffies, Castle Street.

Ray Clemence on the Kop for Liverpool 5 Arsenal 1 sat near a fella who could scarcely believe that he was so close.

Kenny, Marina and Lauren Dalglish having a meal in Steven Gerrard's Warehouse restaurant, Southport.

Celebrity Big Brother runner-up Dappy having breakfast in Soul Cafe, Bold Street.

The entire Crystal Palace squad, most shivering with their hoods pulled up, wandering up Brook Street in the rain.

Pete Price stuck on a delayed London to Liverpool Virgin Train at Milton Keynes station, which forced him to miss his Radio City show.

Desperate Scousewife Amanda Harrington putting money into a pay and display machine on Old Hall Street before heading into Yoga Hub.

Stuart Pearce arriving at the Halliwell Jones Stadium, Warrington.

Lord Daresbury, complaining that the bread rolls weren't soft enough for his liking, in the owners and trainers bar at Haydock Park Racecourse.

Fabio Borini and girlfriend Erin O'Neill in the ME London Hotel, The Strand.

Bluenose boxer Tony Bellew leaving a pitch at the Goals Soccer Centre, Netherton, after a match with his mates.

Ronnie Moran

Ronnie Moran

Simon Mignolet

Stuart Pearce likes to see players carrying a ball under their arm

shopping in Sainsbury's, Crosby.

Simon Mignolet packing shopping into his car outside Tesco, Allerton.

John Aldridge walking up Old Hall Street on his way to Shenanigans pub, Tithebarn Street.

Under-21s defender Lloyd Jones sitting on a chair in the reception of the West Tower building, Brook Street.

Daniel Agger getting into his car in the Capital Car Park, Liverpool city centre.

Jordan Henderson driving a red Range Rover past Dobbie's garden centre, Southport.

Danny Sturridge, wearing a t-shirt with a pig's head on, buying three packets of Carr's table water biscuits in Tesco, Old Hall Street.

Former Everton skipper Mick Lyons enjoying being the centre of attention in the White Star, Mathew Street.

Liverpool-supporting actress Malandra Burrows, aka Kathy in Emmerdale, in the Holdi Indian restaurant, Woolton Village.

Hairy Biker Dave Myers eating noodles in Nam-Po, London Euston Station.

Luis Suarez taking his daughter for a swimming lesson and posing for photos with delighted young Liverpool fans in the David Lloyd Centre, Speke.

John Henshaw, aka Early Doors landlord Ken, on the other side of the bar in the Roscoe Head, Roscoe Street.

Take a look at Tina

The broadcaster arriving at Platform One is Colin Murray

Arsenal legend Franny Jeffers driving down Riverside Drive in an Audi A6.

Juan Mata having a meal in Gusto, Albert Dock.

St Helens RLFC full-back Jonny Lomax ordering four bacon, four eggs, beans and a Malteaser milkshake while having lunch with his team-mates in Bocboc Cafe, St Helens.

Ray Houghton and Colin Murray at Norwich Station.

Jan Molby walking through the away end at Carrow Road.

Aine Coutinho, Philippe's wife, amongst the travelling Kop at Carrow Road.

Ian Ayre driving up Scottie Road in a Bentley.

Brendan Rodgers having a meal in San Carlo, Castle Street.

Tina Malone, aka Mimi Maguire from Shameless, walking into the Radisson, Old Hall Street.

Steven and Alex Gerrard eating in Elif Turkish BBQ restaurant, Lark Lane.

Jose Enrique and his missus dining in Gaucho on St Mary's Street, Manchester.

Steve McManaman at a launch night at posh tailors Gieves and Hawkes, Met Quarter.

You've done Fab there, Borini

It takes two Danny

After Waltzing through last season with his usual partner Luis Suarez, Danny Sturridge could only watch as the latino legend Sambaed off to Brazil for a bit of World Cup action before deciding to Foxtrot off to Spain to play for Salsalona. Danny loves being at a club that have won it Jive times, but doing the wriggly arm dance on his own just isn't as much fun. He's tried doing the Mambo with Rickie Lambo and the Tango with Mario, but the best people to judge who his next partner should be might be found on Strictly Come DANcing...

Solicitors

SLIP, trip or fall? Ended up on your Arsene again? Tired of being hit for five or six? Is it never your fault? We can blitz you in 20 minutes. No compensation. Call Rodgers and Co Solicitors.*

* This publication reserves the right to ignore famous incidents of people slipping over since April 2014

Birthdays

32 Today
YAYA TOURE

To Yaya. Have a lovely day. From Yaya (well, no-one else will bloody say it)

100 Today
YAKUBU & SAMUEL ETO'O

Enjoy your joint birthday party. Don't exhaust yourselves blowing all the candles out! Love from Auntie Maureeno xxx

Vanishing spray

HANDY GADGETS

Spray the past away

You saw it during the World Cup and you're seeing it again now. Vanishing spray is all the rage and it's got more uses than you think. It's not just for helping players realise how far nine* yards is!

*When was the last time you saw a ref actually pace out a full 10 yards?

LFC manager list
Shankly
Paisley
Fagan
Dalglish

Evans
Houllier
Benitez

Dalglish
Rodgers

TVs

BALLO Telly for sale. Difficult to move. Complicated controls. Drama every day. Many previous owners.

Refreshments

LAMBORINI is the perfect drink for the big occasion. Combining the best attributes of two striking sensations. May go flat soon after opening.

Betting

BET 6-4-0

Live odds available

How many shots will West Ham have on target?
6 4/1
4 2/1
0 Evens

Spend your winnings in the Big Sam Casino. Roll the Allar-dice and if you win you've got every right to be big-headed!

Pharmaceutical

TIRED of being a Little Phil? Would you prefer to be known as a Big Phil? Try new G-Force viagra. You'll be big and hard in no time. Then you'll just have to get used to hearing Countinho-o-my!

ADVERT

STEVIE LAX®
'You'll definitely go again'

UNFLAVORED
POWDER
GREE FREE

Warning: Seeing a Man Shitty may cause irritation

38 doses a season   NET WT 17.9 OZ (510g)

Reds fans were left frustrated by a lack of signings in the January 2014 transfer window, particularly when talks with Yevhen Konoplyanka came to nothing. At least Ian Ayre got a few new commercial partners on board in the meantime...

THE KOP MOLE'S PAPARAZZI PICS

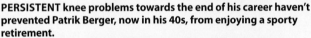

The Kop Mole brings you more of his favourite celeb snaps from 2014

PERSISTENT knee problems towards the end of his career haven't prevented Patrik Berger, now in his 40s, from enjoying a sporty retirement.

The former Liverpool midfielder and fellow ex-Red Vladimir Smicer reportedly turned out for Czech sixth-tier side Dolni Chabry on an occasional basis and Paddy has now taken up snowboarding, tweeting this snap of himself on the slopes of Zauchensee, Salzburg in the Austrian Alps.

Clearly living in England made quite an impact on Berger as most British footballers also spend their retirement on the piste... or at least on a pub sign in the case of Tommy Smith when a consortium headed by him bought the Sutton Manor pub next to the old Sutton Colliery in St Helens and named it after the Anfield Iron.

The downturn in pub trade meant there was never going to be a Smicer Manor when Vladi retired, but maybe Paddy should open a Berger Bar in Prague...

TWERKING used to be what wools in employment did from 9-5, but now it's a form of dance probably best made famous by Miley Cyrus at the MTV Music Awards.

She's got nothing on Colin Pascoe's son Tyler, though, who proved he can shake his backside with the best of them.

Quite what his dad thinks though is anyone's guess as Colin Pascoe would never, ever, ever be seen in public doing such an outrageous thing as...not wearing shorts.

HERE'S a photo of a sexy old Scouse bird who has been associated with men from all over the city.

Also pictured is Mossley Hill-born Liverpool-supporting actress Kim Cattrall (left) who was spotted on a matchday in this number, seemingly just as infatuated with the fittest bird on the planet as the rest of us...

AFTER Danny Sturridge posted these pictures on Twitter, the Daily Mail said he had "questionable fashion sense."

Studge got away lightly. Imagine if they'd seen what he was wearing as a change strip in 2013/14!

BRENDAN Rodgers' Liverpool like to out pass teams so perhaps it was no surprise that he turned up at the ECHO Arena to watch Tinie Tempah perform Pass Out and his other hits.

Tinie even changed the lyrics of his Miami 2 Ibiza hit to Liverpool 2 Ibiza before meeting the Reds boss backstage the night after April's 2-1 win at West Ham.

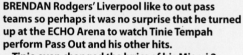

HAVING Phil Jones playing in front of them must take its toll on the eyes, so Man United keepers David de Gea and Anders Lindegaard must be delighted to go home to their stunning girlfriends every night.

De Gea's blonde missus, Edurne Garcia, pictured here modelling United's away kit for next season, is a singer and actress while Lindegaard's Cindy Crawford lookalike lass Misse Beqiri is a Swedish model – the only decent catches both players have ever made.

Wonder if Jim Leighton is sat at home thinking he could've bagged a hottie himself if only he hadn't spent his entire career with his eyebrows coated in Vaseline?

WHEN I heard a Liverpool player had been pictured getting his cock out I feared another Don Hutchison scandal was about to break, but thankfully Joe Allen's bud is a lot less offensive.

The Welsh midfielder has already got four hens – making his £15m signing from Swansea quite a coup – so his chick, sorry, fiancée Lacey-Jo Hughes hatched a plan to buy him a (Glen) cockerel for his 24th birthday.

Joe has called the rooster Bruce – presumably because it's got red hair and a funny nose like Steve – and reportedly celebrated his birthday by having a night out with his team-mates plus WAGs on the Friday before the Reds' 3-0 thrashing of the Mancs last March.

Eggcellent timing I'd say because every Kopite inside Old Trafford was somewhere between cock-a-hoop and clucking delighted that afternoon...

NEVER A GOOD SIGN

Having changed their crest more often than Samuel Eto'o changes club, Everton didn't bother putting the new one on the side of their Main Stand this season, instead opting to plaster a giant image of Roberto Martinez up there alongside the slogan 'Solo Lo Mejor' (only the best). Quite why they moved away from 'Nil Satis Nisi Optimum' (nothing but the best is good enough) is a mystery given that Goodison Park was built around the same time Latin was invented, but if you know your history it's enough to make your heart go 'they'll be changing that again next summer'. We take a look at some of the alternative designs the Blues could've selected...

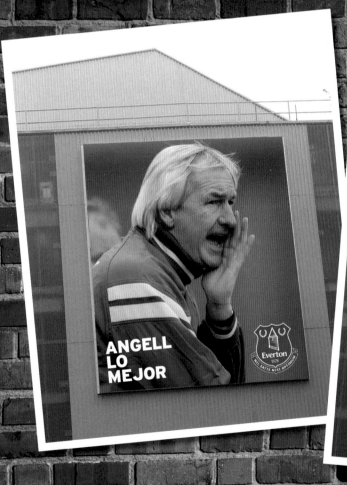

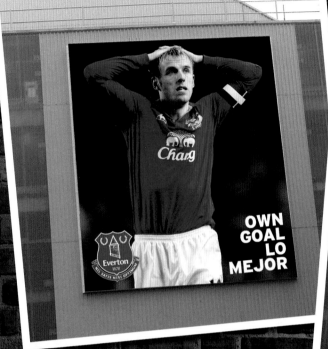

OWN
GOAL
LO
MEJOR

UNITED
LO
MEJOR

SOLO
LO
SAVIOUR

DILDO
LO
MEJOR

The Liverpool FC Winter Olympics

The eyes of the world may have been trained towards the icy surroundings of Sochi in 2014, but the competition we're all interested in was happening in Stocky (Village that is). The Liverpool FC Winter Olympics has been taking place, including some very special events. And unlike Vladimir Putin's Games, we embrace everyone. The only Gueye that's not allowed to watch is Magaye

Curling

Two-man Bob (featuring Paisley and Bolder)

Speedie Skating

KoncheSki Jumping

Ice Jocky

As Liverpool attempted an all-out attacking assault on the 2014 Premier League title you could forgive Brendan Rodgers for playing to his side's strengths. You might want to get round to putting a defence back on the table at some point though boss...

THE KOP MOLE

Digging out the best of the Kop goss and dirt on our rivals from 2014...

INDONESIAN REDS SHOW THEY'VE GOT FLARE

SANTI C said to Stevie G have you heard of The Emirates hospitality? Ste said no, I don't think so, but I've heard of the Indy Reds' pyro.

And here it is. While Anfield was erupting during Liverpool's 5-1 thrashing of Arsenal, there were amazing scenes inside a bar in Bandung.

With several LFC flags on display, including a Spirit of Shankly inspired 'Against Mod£rn Football' banner, Indonesian Kopites turned the air red with a #NoPyroNoParty celebration that was captured by @LFCPhotoIndo.

If they've got a smoking ban in the pubs over there then it isn't going well...

The Famous Kop hikes

ACCORDING to a survey by the Football Supporters Federation, travelling Kopites had the second worst 'away fan experience' in the Premier League in 2013/14.

Supporters were asked to rate all aspects of travelling away and with the day/time of kick off, the cost of match tickets and travel expense ranking as three of the four most important factors when fans choose whether to follow their team it's hardly a surprise that Liverpudlians, who are constantly ripped off by clubs charging higher prices than they do for opponents because they're playing the Reds, felt so dissatisfied.

At the other end of the table, Cardiff and Swansea fans were the happiest to travel away.

Which doesn't say a lot for South Wales.

Reds become feeder club

AT £25 the official Liverpool FC bird feeder isn't cheap, but then following our Liver Bird is an increasingly expensive business.

The Reds marketing department have clearly missed a trick by not asking club ambassador Ian Thrush to tweet about it, but at least the LFC branding should prevent any blue tits from turning up in your garden.

I can also reveal that the Anfield club store received an order for a Liverpool bird feeder from a bored pensioner in Wilmslow.

Apparently he sits in his garden all day trying to knock off anything that lands on the f*****g perch.

UNITED'S CONFECTION DEJECTION

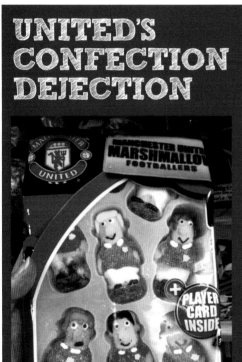

88g℮   8 Hand Decorated Marshmallow Characters

LOUIS van Gaal, as part of his lengthy 'getting my excuses in early' pre-season campaign, claimed the Man United squad he inherited was "broken," so maybe he should've pick players from the marshmallow version instead.

Ruud van Nistelhorse appears to have returned and although Antonio Valencia looks shocked at his green rinse I can honestly say that Phil Jones has never looked better...

Chelsea Football Club
Superb away support as always

Chelsea Football Club's photos in Cardiff City 1-2 Chelsea · Yesterday at 05:29 · 👍

Blue is the colour... of other clubs too

CHELSEA paid tribute to their fans on the final day of the season by uploading this Facebook picture...of Cardiff City supporters.

If seeing 'Cardiff City FC' on the scarves didn't give it away that they weren't Chelsea fans then surely the lack of plastic flags should've done?

CALM DOWN DAVIE

CELTIC'S official matchday programme 'hoops' unearthed this gem from 1982 ahead of their SPFL game against Kilmarnock – David Moyes talking about his rock n' roll lifestyle during his days at Parkhead.

"On Fridays I hire a video tape and stay at home," he said. "The video recorder is one wonder of modern science and plays a big part in my life."

Quite how long it took Dithering Davie to pick a movie to watch is unclear, but he mentioned 'One Flew Over The Cuckoo's nest' – a film about a mental institution run by an abusive, oppressive, power-hungry boss who uses intimidation tactics to keep others in line.

No-one can accuse him of not preparing properly for replacing Fergie at Manchester United then...

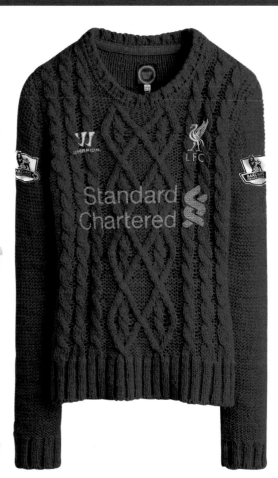

SCOUSERS TURNING INTO WOOLS

Things got so bad at Old Trafford in 2014 that opponents – like Luis Suarez – thought they could turn up wearing knitted boots and still win there. As if he didn't already get enough needle. The adidas-made boots seemingly gave Warrior an idea and we exclusively revealed early designs of Liverpool's 2014/15 kit, before they put those tacky white lines on it anyway...

New Warrior factory opened to cope with production of new kit

Preview of new away kit reveals revolutionary way of exploding the rhombus

Suitably-named Warrior ambassador backs new kit

Link-up with ewe feeder club also set to be announced

The re-emergence of the
wing-heeled Raheem Sterling
throughout 2013/14 was
music to our ears

Chelsea Girl
(with apologies to Aqua)

Hi Chelsea,
Hi Tarquin,
Do you wanna jump on the bandwagon?
Sure Tarquin!
Jump in...

I'm a Chelsea girl, in a Chelsea world,
Flags are plastic, they're fantastic!
Wave them in the air, take them
everywhere.
Imagination? They're not my creation.

Come on Chelsea, you've no history.

I'm a Chelsea girl, in a Chelsea world,
Flags are plastic, they're fantastic!
Wave them in the air, take them everywhere.
Imagination? They're not my creation.

I'm a dumb Chelsea girl, in a plazzy flag
world,
Pick them up, from my seat, every Satdee.
Score a goal, rock 'n roll, to Roman we all
drink,
Wave them here, wave them there, we're
so plastic.
You all laugh, when we wave...
Just cos yours are homemade.

I'm a Chelsea girl, in a Chelsea world,
Flags are plastic, they're fantastic!
Wave them in the air, take them everywhere.
Imagination? They're not my creation.

Come on Chelsea, you've no history,
(Ah-ah-ah-yeah)
Come on Chelsea, you've no history,
(oh no, oh no)
Come on Chelsea, you've no history,
(Ah-ah-ah-yeah)
Come on Chelsea, you've no history,
(oh no, oh no)

Rafa talked, Rafa walked, said whatever
he pleased,
But he won't put a flag, corporate made,
on our seats.
Jose's in, he's our friend, let us wave them
again,
In our ground, there's no sound, it's so quiet
You all laugh, when we wave...
Just cos ours are all club-made.
You all laugh, when we wave...
Just cos yours are all homemade.

Come on Chelsea, you've no history,
(Ah-ah-ah-yeah)
Come on Chelsea, you've no history,
(oh no, oh no)
Come on Chelsea, you've no history,
(Ah-ah-ah-yeah)
Come on Chelsea, you've no history,
(oh no, oh no)

I'm a Chelsea girl, in a Chelsea world,
Flags are plastic, they're fantastic!
Wave them in the air, take them
everywhere.
Imagination? They're not my creation.

I'm a Chelsea girl, in a Chelsea world,
Flags are plastic, they're fantastic!
Wave them in the air, take them
everywhere
Imagination? They're not my creation.

Come on Chelsea, you've no history,
(Ah-ah-ah-yeah)
Come on Chelsea, you've no history,
(oh no, oh no)
Come on Chelsea, you've no history,
(Ah-ah-ah-yeah)
Come on Chelsea, you've no history,
(oh no, oh no)

Oh I'm having so much fun.
Well Chelsea, we've only just got started.
Oh, I love you, Tarquin!

THE KOP KARAOKE

It's Kop Karaoke time, and these three new entries are in a league of their own. Remember – if you play the songs on YouTube (or yer iPod) while reading our re-writes they sound proper boss...

Hope We're Gonna Win A Cup (with apologies to Rick Astley)

I'm no stranger to Lov,
He joined the 'Pool, and so have I.
A Saints contingent's what I'm thinking of,
You wouldn't have got us from any other side.

I just wanna tell you how I'm feeling,
Wanna see our new Main Stand.

Hope we're gonna win a cup,
Try and win back our league crown,
Never let you Kopites down, or desert you.
Hope I'm gonna let one fly,
Maybe even live on Sky,
Gonna have a real good try, to replace Lu.

I've been a Reds fan, for so long,
My heart's been aching, but I'm just tryin'
to say.
Stockport and Rochdale, I was just playin' on,
I've played the game, and now I'm here to
stay.

And, if you ask me how I'm feeling,
Don't tell me you're too blind to see.

That we're gonna win a cup,
Try and win back our league crown
Gonna get a few pennos, and convert you.
Hope I'm gonna let one fly,
Maybe make United cry,
Gonna have a real good try, to replace Lu

Hope we're gonna win a cup,
Try and win back our league crown,
Never let you Kopites down, or desert you.
Hope I'm gonna let one fly,
Now I'm in the number nine,
Gonna have a real good try, to replace Lu

Don't You Worry Like (With apologies to Swedish House Mafia)

There was a time,
You used to put some fear into our eyes.
In your Mancy home,
You were the kings, you had a golden throne.
Those days are gone,
Now they're memories on the wall.
You'll hear the songs,
From the Kopites who've been reborn.

Up Anfield Road the Reds did rewake,
They're making tremors like an earthquake.
I still remember when it all changed.

A Scouser said,
Don't you worry, don't you
worry, like.
See Brendan's got a plan
for you,
Don't you worry, don't
you worry lid, yeah?

In Fergie time,
You had success of a
different kind.
Webb ruled your world,
Thought you'd never

lose, but now you're sh**e.
So now you're done,
We'll think of you now and then.
You'll hear our songs,
Cos Liv'pool will go again.
Up Anfield Road the Reds did rewake,
They're making progress at a fast rate.
I still remember when it all changed.

A Scouser said,
Don't you worry, don't you worry, like
See Brendan's got a plan for you.
Don't you worry, don't you worry lid, yeah?

Oh oh oh oh oh oh-oh
Oh oh oh oh oh oh-oh
Oh oh oh oh oh oh-oh
Oh oh oh oh oh oh-oh
Oh oh oh oh oh oh-oh
Oh oh oh oh oh oh-oh
Oh oh oh oh oh oh-oh...
See Brendan's got a plan for you.

Don't you worry, don't you worry, like.
See Brendan's got a plan for you.
Don't you worry, don't you worry
lid, yeah.

Oh oh oh oh oh oh-oh
Oh oh oh oh oh oh-oh
Oh oh oh oh oh oh-oh... yeah.

Luis Suarez picked up the PFA Player of the Year award in 2014... and another lengthy ban. A transfer ban of their own wouldn't stop Barcelona for signing him for ~~£65million £75million~~ £65million £75million...

THE KOP MOLE'S PAPARAZZI PICS

The Kop Mole brings you more of his favourite celeb snaps from 2014

BRENDAN Rodgers took in a baseball game at Fenway Park during his USA summer holiday where he saw the Boston Red Sox beat the Minnesota Twins 1-0.

Witnessing a home team score just once and keep a clean sheet must've been quite a shock to him.

The Liverpool manager also went gangsta on y'all by wearing three chunky rings on his left hand.

All he needs to do now is get one in the shape of an aeroplane and start drinking out of a Pot Noodle container and he'll look like Sandra from Gogglebox.

EVER been on a night out with non-Liverpool supporting colleagues and got them to pose for a selfie before sneakily reminding them how many European Cups the Reds have won just as the picture is taken?

Phil Thompson has. Although looking at the rest of this 5-a-side team I don't think he'll be winning much else any time soon.

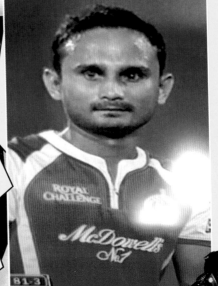

FAT Frank Lampard Junior looks like he's had an Indian or two so here's what he looks like as an Indian.

Ironically I've always thought he's more a fan of chicken tikka than tiki-taka, although the same can't be said about John Terry's (kor)Ma.

She prefers Scouse.

NOT only does Jermaine Pennant have a good agent – how else did he get linked with a move to Napoli? – he's also got himself a rather hot wife.

The former Reds winger married 28-year-old Alice Goodwin at Mere Golf Resort & Spa in May 2014 and uploaded this picture of her on their Seychelles honeymoon to his Instagram account.

Even better than seeing the back of him...

AS if to remind everyone that he did indeed still exist, Jose Enrique posted photos of himself and girlfriend Amy Jaine to his Instagram account on an almost daily basis since the 2013/14 season ended.

We never saw details of his long-term rehabilitation schedule, but if the Liverpool left-back was told to take things easy then he should have made a hell of a recovery – and not before time as it appears he either gets his shorts from the same place Stuart Pearce did in the 1990s or has put on so much weight that none of them fit.

NOTE to Maxi Rodriguez: This possibly wasn't what Argentina coach Alejandro Sabella had in mind when he said he wanted to see a pressing game.

To be fair to the ex-Reds winger you can understand his confusion having previously worked under Roy Hodgson when Liverpool played a depressin' game every week.

I'M not sure if Lucas is planning on starring in a remake of Stephen King's IT or specifically wanted to look like Willy Wonka with a clown's head but he seemed to be enjoying himself with his Queen of Hearts wife Ariana at a fancy dress party in Porto Alegre, Brazil.

Philippe Coutinho also turned up as a Pirate of the Caribbean (well, he was signed by the jolly Rodgers!) while Man Ure defender Rafael gegged in on one photo dressed as Woody from Toy Story.

Quite appropriate really as the Mancs finished (Buzz) Lightyears behind Liverpool in 2013/14 although it's a shame that David Moyes didn't stay in his job to infinity and beyond...

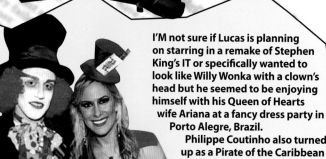

The surprise signing of
Rickie Lambert made him
the seventh LFC player in
England's World Cup squad.
The Roy Hodgson effect
meant the Three Lions would
be a little further away from
the trophy than our new No.9
is in this cartoon

clocked

Yet more celebrities spotted by Kopites including a handful of reality TV stars, Johnny Vegas and John Aldridge eating a baked potato...

Leon and June from Gogglebox

Liz McClarnon

Johnny Vegas

Kumar Sangakkara

Joey Barton, David Nugent, Sean St Ledger and Rob Green in The Ship, Wandsworth – but not sat together.

Kevin Mirallas and his missus leaving the West Tower, home of the Panoramic restaurant.

Mark Lawrenson and family walking a dog down Grosvenor Road, Birkdale.

Gogglebox's heavy-metal loving German Ralph smoking an e-cigarette on St Paul's Square, Liverpool.

Kenny and Marina Dalglish getting off a train at Birkdale Station and strolling arm-in-arm into Bistrot Verite, Liverpool Road, a few moments later.

Rylan Clark carrying books into Villaggio Italian restaurant, Birkdale.

North West Tonight reporter Andy Gill, who has been covering the Hillsborough Inquests brilliantly, shopping in Tesco, Hanover Street.

Peter Crouch and Abby Clancy driving down Lark Lane in a 4x4.

Margi Clarke drinking with friends at the bar in Keiths, Lark Lane.

Phil Neal and David Fairclough dining in San Carlo, Castle Street.

Jennifer Ellison walking down Dale Street with her hair in rollers.

Leon and June Bernicoff, stars of Gogglebox, in the cafe at John Lewis, Liverpool One. We even got a pic!

Phil Thompson watching the FA Cup final in Milly's Wine Bar, Maghull.

Jon Flanagan getting out of a taxi close to Sefton Park.

Ross Barkley driving a black 4x4 close to Otterspool Promenade.

Sri Lankan wicketkeeper Kumar Sangakkara shopping in Zara, Manchester City centre.

Apostolos Vellios taking a suit into Prima dry cleaners, Old Hall Street.

Raheem Sterling in the crowd at Wembley watching former club QPR win promotion against Derby.

Andy Burnham MP walking with his family down Beaumaris Pier in Anglesey.

Jose Enrique partying at the ANTS opening party at Ushuaia Beach Hotel, Ibiza.

Sky Sports' Geoff Shreeves having lunch in Tapas Revolution, Westfield, London.

Paul Ince withdrawing money from the Royal Bank of Scotland ATM, Dale Street.

Everton chief executive Robert Elstone sitting in the sun having a coffee at Cafe Nero, Castle Street.

John Aldridge tucking into a jacket potato with wife Joan (who had a chicken bake) in Costco, Liverpool.

Magaye Gueye, wearing a pair of MC Hammer-style kecks, walking past Challains, Lord Street.

New Hibernian boss Alan Stubbs drinking with friends at Aintree Races.

Phil Neal pushing a trolley full of shopping out of Tesco, Formby.

Gary and Phil (Cockerill & Turner, not Neville), Jordan's stylists, at the Taste of London Festival in Mahiki, Regent's Park, London.

St Helens RLFC prop-forward Kyle Amor walking a dog on Main Street, Billinge.

Brendan Rodgers and former LFC travel manager Charlotte Hind in the Museum of National History, New York.

Former Liverpool winger Tom Ince refusing to have one of those expensive posed pictures taken with his family after walking into Chester Zoo.

British Olympic Gold medallist Katherine Grainger CBE heading into Media City, Salford.

Ex-Blues midfielder Graham Stuart drinking in Villaggio Cucina, Birkdale.

Paul Smith Junior walking past the Liverpool ECHO building, Old Hall Street.

Johnny Vegas driving a VW Golf around the ASDA roundabout, St Helens.

Liz McClarnon at Sefton Park Cricket Club, with a rat-sized dog, watching a charity six-a-side tournament.

Belfast Godfather of punk Terri Hooley drinking in The Parador, Ormeau Road, ahead of a gig in his home city.

Glen Johnson picking up his kid from nursery in Formby.

Book worm: Rylan Clark

Camera shy: Tom Ince

Abby's Larking around

Roller girl Jennifer

Adam Lallalalalalana was Liverpool's most expensive transfer ahead of the 2014/15 season. As if he wasn't under enough pressure also taking on the number 20 shirt after Aly Cissokho!

WORLD CUP
WINNERS:
MESUT OZIL

Jordan Rossiter became Liverpool's second youngest ever goalscorer in September in a routine 74-73 penalty shoot-out victory over Middlesbrough in the Capital One Cup

THE KOP MOLE'S PAPARAZZI PICS

The Kop Mole brings you more of his favourite celeb snaps from 2014

PHILIPPE Coutinho had an oar-some 2013/14 season for Liverpool and spent a day of his summer break doing a spot of canoeing back home in Brazil.

Which was quite ironic as without his creativity in midfield it was only a matter of time before Felipe Scolari's men found their World Cup dream up the creek without a paddle...

CHELSEA midfielder Willian looked delighted when he posted this picture of himself swimming with a dolphin while on holiday in Mexico, but the friendly mammal must have been left feeling a bit perplexed.

It can't be every day it shares the sea with a fella who's got the coral reef on his head...

THE fella who plays James Bond bumped into the fella who plays Austin Powers before Liverpool's pre-season friendly against Man City at Yankee Stadium, New York.

Surely there's a film idea there somewhere?

Whether Kopites Daniel Craig and Mike Myers were indeed discussing the script for a new movie is unclear, but if so it looks like they've already got ex-Fulham boss Felix Magath (say cheese) signed up to play one of the baddies.

MARIO Balotelli's stunning ex-fiancée Fanny Neguesha loves a selfie or two – if you're not following her on Instagram yet then these are the type of photos you're missing out on – and while the last I'd heard was that she'd split with Liverpool's new number 45 their relationship has been on/off so many times over the years that she'll probably turn up at Anfield at some point.

Therefore, it'd be rude of me not to introduce the new WAG on the block properly so here's a handy Fanny fact file.

1. Born and raised in Belgium, Fanny has Rwandan, Congolese and Italian heritage and speaks three languages – Italian, English and French.

2. She has a 'your love is the only thing that makes me love' tattoo on her left arm with Mario's name written underneath.

3. In April 2013 Fanny and Mario appeared on the front cover of Vanity Fair Italia.

4. The Daily Mail are obsessed with what she wears and recently advised readers they can get the 'chic pair of distressed white denim shorts' she was papped wearing for a reduced £14.99 at Topshop.

5. 68% of blokes looking at this page haven't read any of the above four points, they're still looking at Fanny's selfies.

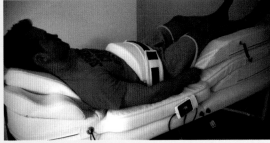

LIVERPOOL keeper Simon Mignolet tweeted this photo of himself using a HHP Andumedic therapy system to help his 'recovery' between games. Or was he just having a lie down on a posh hospital bed wearing a massive bum-bag with his goalie gloves inside it?

GLEN Johnson's form was so poor in 2014 that I've been wondering if an imposter has been wearing the number two shirt and now it appears that I could be onto something.

The Liverpool right-back's family, friends and team-mates threw a surprise 30th birthday party for him and all turned up wearing masks with his mug on.

Which was nice, but maybe if they'd got him one with Jon Flanagan's face on he'd be playing better?

MANAGING Manchester United took a toll on David Moyes – he had so many worry lines on his forehead by the end that Juan Mata could've played between them – and it doesn't appear to be doing Louis van Gaal any favours either.

The Dutchman was spotted looking the worse for wear on the train after a trip to the barbers to dye his hair red.

How long until Wayne Rooney asks to meet him in a hotel room?

GUESS THE GOAL

EUROPEAN CUP SPECIAL

To celebrate Liverpool's return to the UEFA Champions League in 2014, we've picked a dozen European LFC goals and recreated them in Football Manager-style graphic form. How many do you remember? The managers will give you a clue of the era a goal is from, and we've given you an easy starter. *This now could be interesting...*

KEY
- ○ Start
- ● LFC player
- ◐ Opposition player
- ● Opposition keeper
- — Shot path
- -- Ball movement
- Player movement

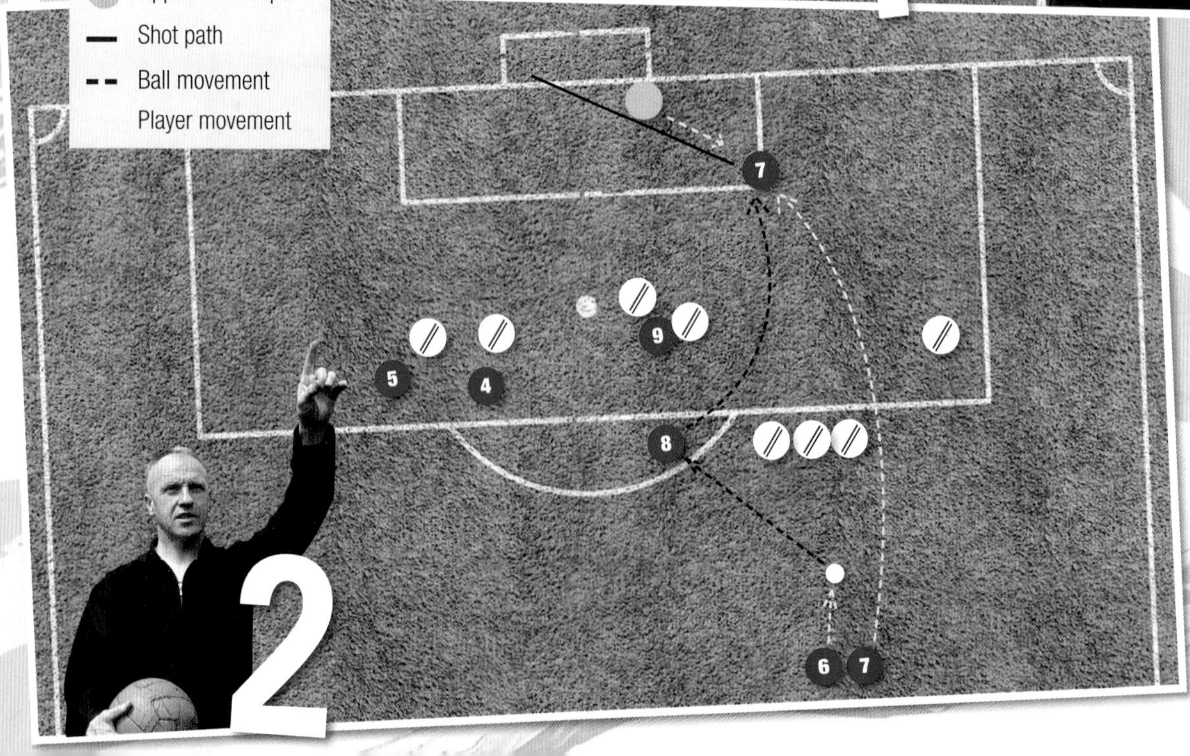

1

2

LFC player

7

8

9

10

And just in case
Thursday nights
are on the agenda
in 2015...

12

11

Dejan Lovren joined Liverpool from Southampton - where else - having established his own online clothes shop. Hopefully his arrival will make it a closed shop in our defence once more...

RODGERS DENIES THAT HIS POLICY OF BUYING SAINTS HAS GONE JUST TOO FAR

clocked

The final instalment of celebrities spotted over the past year, including Tiger Woods, Luke Skywalker and Timmy Mallett

Timmy Mallett

Emre Can viewing Soto Kyrgiakos' penthouse suite in the West Tower, Brook Street.

John Aldridge watching Wilko v Liverpool Quick Boys in the Edge Hill Junior Under-8s league at Botanic Park, Edge Lane.

Suso strolling down the Pier Head with his girlfriend.

Former Reds full-back Fabio Aurelio shopping in the Nike Store at Liverpool One.

Fabio Aurelio with his family in Costa Coffee, Speke Retail Park.

Ex-Everton defender John Bailey walking down Dale Street carrying a plastic bag.

Former Wide Awake Club and Wacaday presenter Timmy Mallett and his son wandering around The Beatles Story, Albert Dock.

Tiger Woods outside the Radisson Blu hotel on Old Hall Street.

Fabio Borini leaving the Hope Street Hotel.

Scouse actor Paul McGann showing a mate around Mathew Street.

Everton new boy Muhamed Besic having a meal sitting outside San Carlo, Castle Street.

Former Everton left-back Michael Ball driving a Range Rover down Altcar Road, Formby, near to the Tesco.

Reds supporting actor Clive Owen in San Carlo on the weekend the giants were roaming around Liverpool.

Nicholas Lyndhurst

Elvis Costello strolling around the Albert Dock with wife Diana Krall and their kids.

Mark Hamill, aka Luke Skywalker, in the Cavern Club, Mathew Street.

Dejan Lovren happily chatting with Liverpool fans outside the Hilton Hotel.

The entire Porto squad milling about the Hilton Hotel.

Usain Bolt partying in Bamboo, Glasgow.

Chris Eubank inside the Hilton Hotel, Park Lane, London.

Strictly Come Dancing's Ola Jordan in pink hot pants at a Farm Foods charity golf day at Nailcote Hall, Warwickshire.

Brendan Rodgers and Commonwealth Games diving gold medallist Tom Daley dining in STK, The Strand, London – although not together.

Martin Skrtel sat in the passenger seat of a car close to Liverpool Cathedral.

Jose Enrique, Suso, Joao Teixeira, Tiago Ilori, Javier Manquillo and their partners having a meal in Australasia, Spinningfield Way, Manchester.

Ross Barkley getting his ears lowered in Cut Throat Pete's Barber Store in Liverpool city centre.

Paul Barber, aka Denzil from Only Fools and Horses and star of One Night In Istanbul, walking towards Cressington Esplanade, Aigburth.

Jose Enrique with family and friends outside John Lewis, Liverpool One.

Tina Malone, aka Mimi Maguire from Shameless, shopping in River Island, Church Street.

Martin Skrtel

Mike McCartney, aka Mike McGear, looking through the window of an empty shop with a couple of women at the top of Bold Street.

Bury striker and long-time Kopite Ryan Lowe collecting tickets from the kiosk next to the Anfield main entrance ahead of the Reds' first home game of the season.

Swansea midfielder Jonjo Shelvey signing autographs and having photos taken with Liverpool fans in the Main Stand car park.

Huddersfield midfielder Conor Coady heading into the Main Stand through a turnstile.

West Bromwich Albion manager Alan Irvine walking into the Anfield directors' and officials' entrance.

Mark Hamill

Alberto Moreno, Javi Manquillo, Jose Enrique and Suso having a meal with their partners in San Carlo, Castle Street.

Raheem Sterling and Jordon Ibe getting on a Virgin train to London.

Nicholas Lyndhurst, aka Rodney Trotter, aka Dave, having breakfast in the Village Urban Resort, Bury.

Andi Peters chatting with former Rangers defender Gordon Ramsay in a cafe at Borough Market, Southwark.

Luis Suarez shopping in Next, New Mersey Retail Park, Speke, on transfer deadline day after visiting Melwood to say goodbye...

Tom Daley

Ola-la!

I hope he's not a Bolt from the Blues

WE GO (BUT DON'T SEE) THE GAME

For the first time since 2002/03 the opening Merseyside derby of the season was at Anfield, meaning Blues attending the match were actually able to see what was happening on the pitch*, a luxury they're not afforded in certain parts of the Theatre of Beams judging by these photos Evertonians were tweeting of Goodison's greatest obstructed views…

*er, unless they ended up in this seat in the Annie Road End (which most of them must wish they'd been sat in for the 4-0 thrashing last season)…

More of the best five-fingered salutes from another set of well-travelled Kopites

Jeff on the front line

WITH the mass media focusing on Liverpool's SAS, Kopite Jeff Canning decided to get a bit retro and remind us of the days when we had the RAF leading the Reds' line.

Roy Evans preferred the RAF (Rush and Fowler) to the CAR (Clough and Rush) when he first took charge, although a few years later his midfield options of Thomas, Walters and Thompson left something to be desired while we should all be thankful that a Dundee, Ince, Carragher, Kvarme back four was never opted for.

Part of RAF Consigby, Jeff is serving at Kandahar Airfield (KAF) in Afghanistan with the 451 EAMXS Reaper Squadron, although it's unclear whether EAMXS is an acronym or was named by some fella who failed his English GESCs.

English is a strange language – why is abbreviation such a long word and how cruel was it to put a letter S in lisp? – but at least it is spoken in most parts of the world with notable exceptions including China, Honduras, Ethiopia and Bradford. We're not entirely sure what type of plane Jeff took The Kop Challenge in front of, but judging by the lack of windows and no obvious facilities it is probably operated by Ryanair.

from **Kandahar Airfield, Afghanistan**

Frosty reception for Reds fans

ICELAND is one of the most difficult countries in Europe to travel around in – try programming a SatNav for Hafnarfjörður and Reykjanesbær – but The Kop has made it to the frozen food specialist country.

Paul Hogan and Kevin Walsh gave a five-fingered salute with The Kop Annual at Gullfoss, a waterfall located in the Canyon of Hvítá that famously appeared on the front cover of 'Porcupine', an album by Echo and the Bunnymen.

Ian McCulloch and co had planned to get the photo in Scotland but were concerned about a lack of snow so went to Gullfoss instead where photographer Brian Griffin described it as "difficult to stand up."

Had they gone to Scotland they'd have experienced similar difficulties at pub closing time and had they visited the part of Edinburgh that Trainspotting was filmed in they'd also have seen plenty of the white stuff.

Volcanos aren't the only danger in Iceland and the boys were thankful that when they encountered this polar bear it was stuffed, possibly because it had been for a meal in the Tjobyy Cjarveryy. Seconds after this photo was taken of the bear looking all grizzly and frightening it shook paws with the lads and nuzzled up to them. They now believe it was bipolar.

from **Canyon of Hvita, Iceland**

Fun in (but not with) the s*n

SHANKLY'S bar in Salou is not just somewhere to drink in while on holiday – it's much more important than that – and is a popular place for Kop Challenge entries.

It's not the only bar in Salou that is named after a football manager, although we've yet to see a single five-fingered salute in The Purple Nose, Myopic Frenchman or Big Fat Sam's.

Taking The Kop Challenge was Birkenhead-based Lee Sutton with his wife Sheree, son Rob and daughters Jade and Lily who were joined by Shankly's landlord and landlady Chris and Dotty.

Now in its 10th year, Shankly's has got more European Cups on display than Everton and welcomes non-Liverpool supporters, but a certain newspaper is completely banned, making it the only part of the Med where you won't find the s*n.

Although Shankly's has been successful, other football themed bars in Spain haven't done as well.

'Bar Wigan' is only ever a quarter full, 'The Coventry' was moved to a completely different location 34 miles away for a while, it costs £60-a-pint in 'The Arsenal' and drinkers in 'The White Hart' aren't allowed to use the Y-word, making life tough for Tottenham fans who can't help but yawn when watching their team play.

from **Salou, Spain**

Bill breaks new ground for Kop Challenge – two new places to be Pacific

WE'VE no idea why Danny Welbeck is so popular on Easter Island but they appear to have put a giant statue of him up there.

Welbeck, son of bomb disposal expert Stan, has the squarest haircut in the Premier League and only needs to grow it by a further four inches to qualify as a member of the Queen's Guard.

Liverpool supporter Bill Redfearn, an ex-pat from Aigburth now living in Canada, spotted the Welbeck monument during a South Pacific cruise and gave a five-fingered salute, although judging by the lack of a smile on the statue's face it hasn't yet heard David Moyes got the sack.

Bill also visited two new Kop Challenge countries starting with French Polynesia, which was named after a Parisian parrot suffering from memory loss. He's pictured with The Kop in Fakarava, a place that sounds as if it doesn't have much time for ex-Middlesbrough striker Fabrizio Ravanelli.

Fakarava only has 855 inhabitants, much like the Riverside Stadium for a Middlesbrough home game these days, but it's fair to say the blue lagoon, white sandy beach and palm trees make it slightly easier on the eye than the grey skies, rows of chimneys and plumes of smog on Teesside.

The Kop also made a debut appearance on the Pitcairn Islands – the last remaining British colony in the Pacific Ocean made up of four islands, the biggest of which is the uninhabited Henderson Island.

Archeologists believe a small settlement lived on the island between the 12th and 15th centuries. The reason for the Hendersonians disappearance is unclear, but the chances are they ran themselves into the ground.

from **Easter Island, Pitcairn Islands and French Polynesia, Pacific Ocean**

A Great Read at the Great Reef

THE Great Barrier Reef, North Queensland is not only very self-congratulatory but it sounds like something Jose Mourinho would stick in front of the Chelsea goal when playing away from home.

We're not saying Jose has negative tendencies, but after calling out a Sky engineer because his remote control wasn't working it was discovered that the batteries inside had minus signs at both ends.

Yawninho's bus parking tactics have been good news for Chelsea financially – they recently struck a deal with Cadbury to make Double Decker the club's official chocolate bar – and the return of Didier Drogba gives them an added physical presence lying on the floor in the box.

Diego Costa's arrival also meant that Fernando Torres was sent on loan to AC Milan - and they thought Mario Balotelli didn't do much running - but the departure of David Luiz was a real blow.

For the rest of the Premier League.

Taking The Kop Challenge down under in a wetsuit, flippers, goggles and snorkelling gear was Kopite Ronan Park.

He didn't get the equipment especially to go swimming in the clear blue water – he's from Belfast originally and it rains a lot there – and made a good decision not to use our iPad edition for this particular photo.

from **North Queensland, Australia**

School away trip 3, School home trip 5

SCHOOL trip destinations have certainly changed during recent times.

Back in the day visits to Colomendy, Speke Hall, Ellesmere Port Boat Museum and, if you went to a really poor school, Wigan Pier was as good as it got, but now football stadiums are on the schedule for kids.

Jack Owen (no relation to Michael) and Ewan Melia (no relation to Jimmy) from Burton-upon-Trent went to Old Trafford for their school trip.

Although travelling up the M6 to get there replicated what it's really like to be a United fan, we called OFSTED after receiving this photo and asked them to launch an urgent investigation to establish just how badly the lads had behaved to be given such a horrific punishment.

At least Ewan and Jack, whose dad Darron sent the picture in, made the most of a bad situation by taking The Kop Challenge in the Mancs' museum. The shirts behind them are due to be replaced by a couple of Howard Webb's next month.

Thankfully their school made amends the following day by sending them to Anfield on a second school trip where they got to see five European Cups and their United-supporting classmates, who asked where the Premier League trophy was, taken down a peg or two by the tour guide.

"What the difference between Man United and Aberystwyth Town?" he said. "Aberystwyth Town are in Europe..."

from **Old Trafford, Salford**

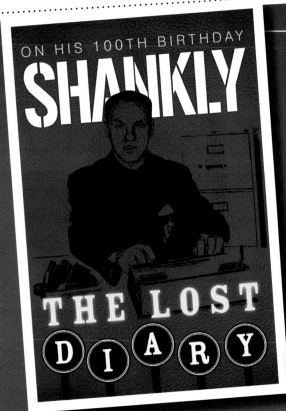
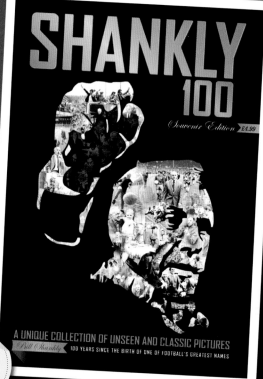

BOB PAISLEY
SMILE ON ME AND GUIDE MY HAND

The updated biography of Liverpool's triple European Cup-winning manager, 40 years after he took the job...

2014 marked the 40th anniversary of the day Bob Paisley took over the Anfield hotseat and his highly-acclaimed authorised biography gives a new generation of Liverpool fans the opportunity to get to know the Anfield legend.

John Keith originally wrote Bob's bestselling life story at the turn of the Millennium and it is viewed by many Kopites as the closest they will ever get to reading the autobiography that Paisley sadly never penned.

With reflections and reminiscences from many other football legends – including Kevin Keegan, Billy Liddell and Alan Hansen – this is the compelling story of Liverpool's reluctant genius, one of the greatest managers the game has ever seen.

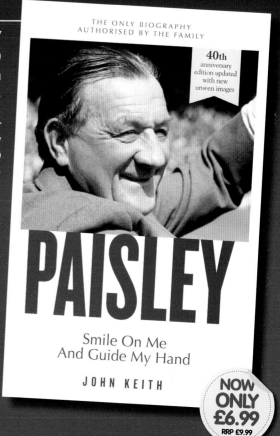

THE ONLY BIOGRAPHY
AUTHORISED BY THE FAMILY

40th anniversary edition updated with new unseen images

PAISLEY

Smile On Me
And Guide My Hand

JOHN KEITH

NOW ONLY £6.99 RRP £9.99

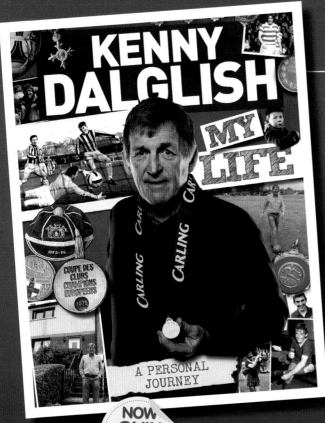

KENNY DALGLISH
MY LIFE
A PERSONAL JOURNEY

NOW ONLY £7.50 RRP £19.99

KENNY DALGLISH
MY LIFE

From his childhood dreams to his prized medals, Kenny's revealing scrapbook...

Imagine spending time with the man officially rated Liverpool Football Club's greatest ever player as he talks you through his career, shows you his favourite medals and shirts, and tells you about the people who helped shape his career.

From King Kenny's childhood dreams, his schoolboy awards and certificates to his European Cup, FA Cup and league title medals, the scrapbook allows Kopites to view his amazing collection of football memorabilia as he talks us through the things that mean most to him.

He also sheds light on his two trophy-laden spells as Liverpool boss – and the managers who inspired him. Any Kopite worth the Liver Bird on his chest will love King Kenny's personal scrapbook.

or call: **0845 143 0001**

Prices subject to change. P&P not included in prices shown. Lines open Monday to Friday 9am-5pm.

The surprise signing of Mario Balotelli
was a gamble... a bit like having a lit
firework inside a suitcase

You Ask, We Answer

✍ I READ last season how Liverpool's players had become mentally stronger by working with 'brain mechanic' Steve Peters.

I don't drive one of those fancy cars but any idea what he charges for a full service and MOT on a 2007 Vauxhall Corsa?

Miss Understood, Tuebrook

A: Looks like you'll need your inner chimp replacing, love, won't be cheap.

✍ FOLLOWING a number of enquiries into my health and wellbeing due to a misunderstanding over my surname, I'd like to set the record straight.

I've never had Ebola.

Dele Adebola, Nigeria

A: Are you sick of playing for crap clubs though?

✍ DURING a visit to a psychic I was told that my deceased father wanted to get a message to me that he once bumped into a Jari Litmanen lookalike in our local newsagents. He was buying 20 Benson & Hedges and a packet of extra strong mints.

Does he win a prize?

Brian Straw-Clutcher Junior, Hants

A: If the psychic was any good you'd already know that he doesn't.

✍ I SAT down to watch LFC TV last night after they advertised a programme called 'Goal Rush'.

Imagine my frustration and disappointment when I found myself viewing a collection of goals from Liverpool's 2013/14 season rather than a tribute show to legendary Welsh marksman Ian Rush who, for my money, is the Reds' greatest striker of all time.

I believe this is the worst case of false advertising since Sky Sports showed highlights of Liverpool's 0-0 draw with Reading on 'Goals on Sunday'.

Ian Rush, Flint

A: Rumour has it some of LFC TV's 'Kop Kids' even sit in the Annie Road end.

✍ MY father is getting on in years and I'm beginning to think he may be losing his mind.

His latest claim is that Dutch international striker Arjen Robben spends his spare time wandering around the streets of Munich dressed as a ghost in an attempt to scare the locals.

Is it time to pack the old man off to a nursing home or what?

Sue So, Tower Hill

A: No. Our picture clearly shows that it isn't just the far post Robben likes to ghost in at.

✍ FAR be it from me to question the skills of maths teachers in Northern Ireland, but I'm beginning to question if Brendan Rodgers wasn't taught basic arithmetic.

In 2009, Southampton Football Club was sold for a reported £15 million yet five years on Rodgers decides it's good business to buy three of their players for £50m.

Plainly it would have been more prudent to purchase the entire football club for £25m, keep the players he wanted and sell the rest off down that big car boot sale at Burscough on a Sunday morning to raise further transfer funds.

Matt Matician, Ormskirk

A: An opportunity to sell a coffee table, two Star Wars figures and Morgan Schneiderlin in the same transaction has evidently been missed by the overpaying LFC boss.

✍ HELLO. I've been a massive Liverpool fan since 2013 and I've started a Twitter page about Alberto Moreno's tattoos including a comprehensive guide to the reason behind each inking. Please can I have a shout out?

Kay Boardwarrior, Belfast

A: No. Please RT.

✍ HAVING reviewed the plans for Liverpool's new Main Stand in some detail and assessed how the building work might affect my matchday experience, I now believe there will be minimal personal impact.

This is largely because I'm a season ticket holder at Exeter City and have never visited Anfield in my life.

Bob Spraghead, Exeter

A: Apologies for the lack of inconvenience caused.

✍ IN 1969 I attended my first Liverpool game at Anfield, a remarkable 10-0 victory against Dundalk in the European Fairs Cup.

I drove to the match in my red Ford Cortina Mark II and parked just off Pinehurst Avenue where a helpful young attendant offered to mind my car for 10 pence.

I was grateful to the lad for taking the worry off my mind that something could happen to my pride and joy, but he's done such a good job that I've yet to receive my car back.

If anyone knows of the vehicle's whereabouts please get in touch as I must owe him a good few quid by now.

E. C. Target, Warrington

A: If you need anyone to mind your wallet next time give us a shout.

✍ I WISH to call into question another one of Bill Shankly's famous quotes.

In his autobiography, first published in 1977, he wrote "An athlete should look like an athlete. His eyes should sparkle so much you could light a cigarette from them."

I've always taken the great man's word as gospel, but having recently started a three-year degree in Sports Science and discussed this matter with my tutor I was informed that if I poked cigarettes into the eyes of the university football team as part of my dissertation I would be thrown off the course for gross misconduct.

I'm beginning to think that Shanks' methods of judging an athlete are no longer relevant in the modern day game.

Eimar Bitslow, Litherland

A: It appears that Shankly's legendary anecdotal tales may have been lost on you.

✍ I'VE read that UKIP leader Nigel Farage wants to cut down on wealthy foreign 'health tourists' coming to Britain to have free treatment on the NHS.

Are we really meant to believe such a scam goes on?

Ed Milliband, Doncaster

A: This evidence from Manchester suggests so.

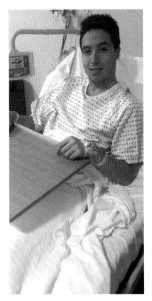

MY granddad reckons that during a particularly ill-tempered Merseyside derby in the 1960s, Liverpool had 10 men sent off for an early bath leaving just Ian St John on the pitch for the final 14 minutes.

He says that despite this the Saint held on for a credible 2-2 draw and came close to nicking a winner when heading his own corner against the post.

Is he having me on?

Will.I.Am Shankly, Scotland

A: He's not. This photo shows the scene in the Liverpool bath after hearing their team-mate had just forced the corner your granddad mentioned.

HAVE you noticed that Adam Lallana is an anagram of 'A Llama Land' if you conveniently get rid of the extra A?

I've been laughing at this for a good 25 minutes.

Colin Wanker, Croydon

A: There's nothing like a funny anagram to make people laugh, eh Neil?

ON returning home from the local bakery I spotted that the muffin I'd purchased looks like a cross between Angel Di Maria and Gary Neville.

As a result I called Rentokil and went hungry.

Emma Teetummy, Cork

A: Rats.

I WISH to complain about the public transport issues affecting the Anfield area on matchdays.

I play bingo on a Monday night but on March 10, 2014, the night Liverpool played Sunderland, I walked to my usual bus stop on Anfield Road to catch a number 28 only to be horrified to see a queue of 5,000 people.

To make matters worse, only one bus came along and instead of anyone getting on it they started cheering and singing as it went past.

I wouldn't have minded missing the bingo if the driver had been doing a particularly good job, but getting applause for driving along at 5mph is a little over the top.

It only goes to show what a bad state our bus service is in.

Miss D Mecca, Anfield

A: You could've gone to the match to see a full house.

IT has taken me five years but I have finally thought of a good song for Glen Johnson.

I'm not telling you what it is though in case anyone else tries to sing it at Anfield before I next attend a match.

I estimate this to be in 2057 as I'm currently 23,618th on the season ticket waiting list.

Warren Arlarse, Garston

A: Can't wait. Glen Johnson may have even rediscovered his form by then.

DO you know what really pisses me off about the press? Other than the way the papers fawn over Jose Mourinho, obviously.

I really hate lazy journalism and poor sub-editing.

Stories are often dragged out to fill space and don't get me started on sub-editors failing to spot that the end of a sentence has fallen off the bottom of the

* **Brought to you in association with the groundsmen who have to carry the spare net Simon Mignolet does his warm-up in down to the Annie Road end before kick-off**

* *LOUIS Van Gaal - take the skipper's armband off Wayne Rooney and appoint Daley Blind as captain instead to ensure the Blind really are leading the blind at Old Trafford.*
Danny Blind, Netherlands

* *REDUCE your iTunes bill by simply playing the same song over the PA System moments before every home game kicks off over a period of 44 years.*
George Sephton, Anfield

* *SAVE your career, reputation and an influx of grey hair by not taking the Manchester United job in the first place.*
David Moyes, no fixed abode

* *DON'T take the writings of Dr Steve Peters too literally. I tried to embrace the 'inner chimp' he speaks of but have since been charged with unlawfully entering an animal enclosure and received a lifetime ban from Chester Zoo.*
Eddie Yot, New Brighton

* *SEX education teachers - please ensure that young Evertonians in your class attend lessons to save them the embarrassment of incorrectly using a large purple sex aid live on Sky TV during transfer deadline night coverage.*
Alan Irwin, Kirkby

* *STEER clear of taking driving lessons with the Iago Aspas School of Motoring. I've been learning with them for nine months and I still can't take a corner.*
Elle Plates, Spain

* *LADIES - think again before telling your husband that you're 'too tired' for sex. I used that excuse last week and before I knew it he was discussing it with the world's media in a press conference.*
Mrs Hodgson, London

* *SAVE a fortune on officially licensed FIFA vanishing spray by simply using white spray paint, available at most local DIY stores, to draw a permanent line on the living room carpet that keeps the missus 10 yards away from the remote control on matchdays.*
R Kidda, Belle Vale

* *WHEN slipping on your fucking arse pray that the ball falls to Edin Dzeko or Leonardo Ulloa, making it far more difficult for rival fans to think of a chant that rhymes.*
Ste Gerrard, Liverpool

* *MAKE football more than a game of two halves by sinking three pints down your local during a 90 minute period when there's a match on.*
Elle Bowbender, Walsall

* *DOCTORS - help patients suffering from insomnia to become less reliant on medication by prescribing a BT Sport subscription with one dose of Michael Owen's co-commentary to be taken twice a week.*
Abdul Asditchwater, Ewloe

* *MAKE an absolute fortune during the football season by acquiring an airfield and private plane close to Salford then waiting for Manchester United supporters to make bookings every time they want their manager sacked.*
N Trepreneur, Barton

* *JAMIE Carragher - jib off playing with touch-screen graphics on the telly and return to Liverpool as a defensive coach after chinning Gary Neville live on air during the half-time analysis of West Brom v Hull.*
B Rodgers, Merseyside

* *EARN yourself a lucrative contract by having a great season on loan before reverting back to being the aging, slow, dirty, one-footed yard dog midfielder that everyone thought you were as soon as you've penned a permanent deal.*
Gareth Barry, Walton

* *MANCHESTER City - make me a fucking birthday cake next year or you can stick your £250,000-a-week where the sun doesn't shine.*
Yaya T, Manchester

* *DISGUISE the fact that you've never been prolific in front of goal from open play by living a wild and crazy lifestyle that catches the attention of the press, distracting them from the bigger issue of trying to replace a 31-goal striker.*
Mario Balotelli, Formby

Exclusive Kop print when you subscribe

Buy yourself a laugh and a great red read every month by subscribing to The Kop Magazine.

We're offering you a 10% discount if you do, and if you live in the UK, we'll throw in an exclusive free A4 print of the Kop doing what it does best...being awesome.

To take advantage of these offers simply visit www.merseyshop.com, call them on 0845 143 0001 or fill in the form and send it to Kop Subs, Sport Media, PO Box 48, Old Hall Street, Liverpool, L69 3EB.

Fancy getting 10% off the cover price?

YOUR DETAILS

Mr/Mrs/Ms/Dr:............. Initial:............. Surname:..

Address:...

....

Zip/postcode:.. Country:..

Tel no:.. Date of Birth:...

email:...

I enclose a cheque/postal order for £ [   ] made payable to **SPORT MEDIA**

KOP yearly subscription prices (prices below include discount)
UK . . . £21.60 + £6.40 p&p = £28   Europe . . . £21.60 + £20.40 p&p = £42   Rest of world . . . £21.60 + £26.40 p&p = £48

* Prices subject to change

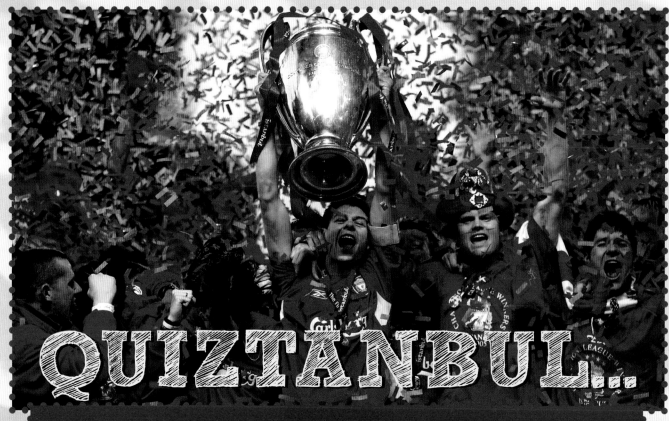

QUIZTANBUL...

2015 marks 10 years since Liverpool's fifth European Cup win, but how much can you remember about that Champions League campaign and the men involved in it? There are 50 questions to answer and if you get all 50 right consider yourself a genius...

The Qualifiers

1. The Reds opened with a qualifying win against Grazer AK, but which actor was their stadium named after?

2. It was Rafa Benitez's first match as Liverpool manager, but can you name his three Spanish backroom staff members who sat on the bench with him that night?

3. Jose Miguel Gonzalez Rey was involved in that match in Austria, but in what capacity? a) Referee b) Played right-back for Liverpool c) Head coach of Grazer AK.

4. Name the unused sub on the Liverpool bench in Graz who left the club four days later.

5. Which Academy graduate started his first ever game for the Reds in the second leg against Grazer AK at Anfield?

6. And which goalkeeper sat on the bench that night for the only time in a Champions League match in his entire career?

7. Who came off the bench to score against Monaco at Anfield in the Reds' 2-0 opening group stage match victory?

8. The player he replaced had earlier netted his first Champions League goal for Liverpool. Who was he?

9. Name the Monaco striker who played in that game and failed to score but went on to net against the Reds for three different clubs between 2008 and 2011.

10. Liverpool's 1-0 defeat to Olympiakos in Athens was refereed by the man who took charge of the 2002 World Cup final. Name him.

11. Who started Liverpool's 0-0 draw with Deportivo La Coruna at Anfield wearing the number 22 shirt?

12. Name the Deportivo defender who put through his own goal in La Coruna to give the Reds a vital 1-0 win.

13. Reds keeper Chris Kirkland was briefly knocked out in Depor after being accidentally 'clotheslined' by one of his team-mates. Which Liverpool player was responsible?

14. Which Liverpool defender needed 20 stitches in a head wound after being substituted just three minutes into the 1-0 defeat away to Monaco?

15. And name the Academy player who started that game to make his Champions League debut, one of two appearances he made in the competition that season.

16. Florent Sinama-Pongolle cancelled out Rivaldo's opener against Olympiakos, but can you recall the name of the island he was born on?

17. Neil Mellor was wearing a blue wristband when he scored against Olympiakos at Anfield, but what cause was he raising awareness for?

18. In which minute of the match did Steven Gerrard score his iconic 'you beauty' winner? a) 84th minute, b) 86th minute, c) 88th minute.

The knock-out stage

19. Name the two players who scored from free-kicks in the Reds' 3-1 last 16 first leg victory against Bayer Leverkusen.

20. Which player appeared for Rafa Benitez for the first time when coming on as a substitute during that match?

21. Three players who went on to play for either Liverpool, Manchester United or Everton appeared for Leverkusen in the last 16 second leg match in Germany. Name them.

22. Name the Liverpool midfielder who came on for the final 20 minutes of the 3-1 win in the Bay Arena in what was the only Champions League appearance of his career.

23. Before the quarter-final first leg against Juventus at Anfield, Kopites held aloft a mosaic featuring an Italian word. What was it, and what did it translate as?

24. Sami Hyypia and Luis Garcia scored for the Reds, but who netted Juve's goal?

25. How many of the Liverpool side beaten 1-0 in the FA Cup at Burnley started in the Champions League quarter-final second leg against Juventus in Turin? A) 1 B) 3 C) 5 D) 8

26. Two future Liverpool players appeared for Chelsea in the semi-final first leg at Stamford Bridge. Name them.

27. Which Liverpool player was suspended for the second leg at Anfield after Eidur Gudjohnsen got him booked by diving?

28. What nationality was referee Lubos Michel who decided Luis Garcia's fourth-minute strike in the second leg at Anfield had crossed the line?

29. Who came on for the physically exhausted Didi Hamann, who was making his first start for almost two months after injury, for the final 18 minutes of the game?

30. How many minutes of injury time were added on at the end of the second half?

Istanbul

31. What date was the Champions League final in Istanbul on?

32. Which team kicked off the first half in the Ataturk Stadium?

33. Only three players appeared in all 15 of Liverpool's Champions League games in 2004/05. Name them.

34. Who was Liverpool's substitute keeper in Istanbul?

35. The referee in Istanbul shared a surname with a player Rafa Benitez later signed for the Reds. What was it?

36. Which Liverpool player conceded the free-kick that Paolo Maldini opened the scoring from?

37. Name the two players who played the passes for Hernan Crespo's goals.

38. Steven Gerrard headed John Arne Riise's cross into the net in the 54th-minute but what shirt number was the Norwegian wearing?

39. Vladimir Smicer added a second after receiving a pass from which Liverpool player?

40. Who was brought down and which AC Milan player committed the foul for the penalty Xabi Alonso netted from the rebound?

41. Did Jerzy Dudek make his wonder save in extra-time with his right or left glove?

42. Who missed AC Milan's first two penalties in the shoot-out?

43. And who scored Liverpool's first two spot-kicks?

44. What was happening behind the goal while Jon Dahl Tomasson took his penalty? A) A flare was being extinguished by a fire marshal B) An ambulance drove past C) An AC Milan fan was being wrestled to the ground by three police officers?

45. Which player got to Jerzy Dudek first to celebrate after he saved Andriy Shevchenko's penalty?

46. Who handed Steven Gerrard the European Cup?

47. What headline did we run on the front of The Kop Magazine the following month? A) Them Scousers Again B) In Istanbul we won it five times C) Ol' Big Ears is ours to keep.

48. Who finished 2004/05 as Liverpool's leading scorer in the Champions League?

49. And which player would've appeared in all 15 matches had he not been an unused sub in the home tie against Grazer AK?

50. What was the official UEFA attendance in the Ataturk Stadium for the Champions League final? A) 72,059 B) 75,055 C) 76,183 D) 79,498

ANSWERS: 1. Arnold Schwarzenegger; 2. Pako Ayestaran, Paco Herrera, Jose Ochotorena; 3. B – but he was better known as Josemit; 4. Michael Owen; 5. Darren Potter; 6. Paul Harrison; 7. Milan Baros; 8. Djibril Cisse; 9. Emmanuel Adebayor; 10. Pierluigi Collina; 11. Chris Kirkland; 12. Jorge Andrade; 13. Igor Biscan; 14. Josemi; 15. Neil Mellor; 16. Réunion; 17. Anti-bullying campaign; 18. A) 84th; 19. John Arne Riise & Didi Hamann; 20. Anthony Le Tallec; 21. Andriy Voronin, Dimitar Berbatov, Landon Donovan; 22. John Welsh; 23. Amicizia/friendship; 24. Fabio Cannavaro; 25. C) 5 (Dudek, Hyypia, Traore, Nunez, Biscan); 26. Glen Johnson and Joe Cole; 27. Xabi Alonso; 28. Slovakian; 29. Harry Kewell; 30. Six; 31. May 25, 2005; 32. Liverpool; 33. Jamie Carragher, John Arne Riise, Sami Hyypia; 34. Scott Carson; 35. Gonzalez; 36. Djimi Traore; 37. Andriy Shevchenko & Kaka; 38. Six; 39. Didi Hamann; 40. Steven Gerrard was brought down by Gennaro Gattuso; 41. Right (although the ball may have brushed a finger tip on his left glove first); 42. Serginho and Andrea Pirlo; 43. Didi Hamann; 44. B) An ambulance drove past; 45. Jamie Carragher; 46. Lennart Johansson; 47. A) Them Scousers Again; 48. Luis Garcia; 49. Steve Finnan; 50. A) 72,059.